A Kick
In The Seat
Of The Pants

"In *A Whack on the Side of the Head* we looked at getting ideas through play; in *A Kick in the Seat of the Pants* we look at the four roles of the creative process. It is a powerful idea."
> —Bob Metcalfe,
> Chairman, 3Com Corp.

"*Kick*'s made my people more creative, and it's a lot of fun to boot."
> —Bill Samuels,
> President, Maker's Mark Distillery

"Hard-hitting and practical approaches to becoming more innovative."
> —Doug King,
> Vice President, American
> Electronics Association

A Kick In The Seat Of The Pants

Using Your Explorer, Artist, Judge & Warrior To Be More Creative

Roger von Oech

Illustrated by George Willett

PERENNIAL LIBRARY

Harper & Row, Publishers
New York, Cambridge, Philadelphia, San Francisco
London, Mexico City, São Paulo, Singapore, Sydney

A KICK IN THE SEAT OF THE PANTS.
Copyright © 1986 by Roger von Oech

Library of Congress Cataloging-in-Publication Data

Von Oech, Roger.
A kick in the seat of the pants.

Bibliography: p.
Includes index.
1. Creative thinking. 2. Success. I. Title.
BF408.V579 1986 153.3'5 85-45238
ISBN 0-06-015528-0 86 87 88 89 90 2001 MPC 10 9 8 7 6 5 4 3 2 1
ISBN 0-06-096024-8 (pbk.) 86 87 88 89 90 2001 MPC 10 9 8 7 6 5 4 3 2 1

Design: George Willett

Typestyle: ITC Cheltenham Light, set by Frank's Type, Mountain View, California

For Information about Creative Think: Box 7354 Menlo Park, California 94026

To Wendy, Athena & Alexander

Table of Contents

Preface

Winter, Spring, Summer, Fall
East, West, North, South
Earth, Air, Fire, Water
Matthew, Mark, Luke, John
Freshman, Sophomore, Junior, Senior
Lethargy, Busyness, Timidity, Arrogance
War, Famine, Pestilence, Death
Soprano, Alto, Tenor, Bass
First, Second, Third, Home
Length, Breadth, Depth, Time
Explorer, Artist, Judge, Warrior

Several years ago, I wrote a book called *A Whack on the Side of the Head.* Its basic idea was that we're all born with the ability to think about things in original ways, but as we grow up we develop attitudes that undermine this creativity. They include: "to err is wrong," "don't be foolish," "that's not my area," "be practical," and "follow the rules." These attitudes make sense for much of what we do, but when we try to generate new ideas, they imprison our imaginations. For this reason, I called them *mental locks,* and provided some tips to open them. *Whack* struck a responsive chord, and I received many comments and ideas from readers from around the world.

This book, *A Kick in the Seat of the Pants,* represents my continuing study of the creative process. Its basic idea is that there's not just one type of thinking, but a variety. To be successful as a creative thinker, you need to adopt a different creative thinking role during each stage of the creative process. *Kick* is about these different roles.

The title of this work, like that of its predecessor, reflects my belief that once a person has settled into a comfortable routine, he needs extraordinary measures to make him get up and say, "I'm going to try something different."

I'd like to thank the following people who shared their ideas with me: Doug King, Jim Hornthal, Bob Wieder, Wiley Caldwell, Mitch Kapor, Dave Liddle, Mary Granius, Kathy Seligman, Lance Shaw, Nancy Parker, Bob Metcalfe, Alan Cooper, Linda Vlasic, Jack Grimes, Jean Caldwell, Nick Zirpolo, Doug Modlin, Bill Samuels, Bryan Mattimore and Scott Love.

I also appreciate the help of Grid Systems. (*Kick* was written on a Grid computer.)

Special thanks to Bill Shinker and Harriet Rubin at Harper & Row.

Hearty appreciation to George Willett for his illustrations.

Most of all, I'd like to thank my family—my wife and editor Wendy, my four year old daughter Athena (who suggested that I call this book *A Kick in the Seat of the Dress*), and my son Alexander—for the support they've given me during this project.

Roger von Oech
Halloween, 1985
Menlo Park, California

Jack's Visit To The Idea Doctor

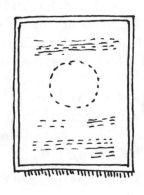
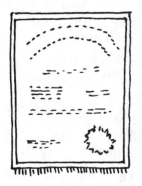
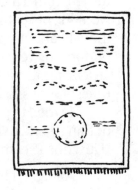

Jack's Visit To The Idea Doctor

People who are resting on their laurels are wearing them on the wrong end.

—Malcolm Kushner, Philosopher

Jack's mind felt like a head of wilted lettuce. He'd just returned from a meeting with his boss, and had found out that he wouldn't be getting the promotion he'd been hoping for. As he thought about his situation, Jack realized that he hadn't been performing very well lately. He had missed deadlines on several crucial projects. And his once perceptive mind was producing trite solutions to important problems.

He tried to put some pizzazz back into his thinking, but nothing worked. Finally, he went to an idea doctor for help. "I just don't seem to have it anymore," Jack explained.

"All right, I'll ask you a few questions so I can figure out what your problem is," the idea doctor responded. "First, have you stuck your neck out and taken any risks lately?"

"Not that I can remember," Jack answered.

"Have you been asking 'what if?' to stretch your imagination?"

"I've been too busy."

"Have you kept an open mind when evaluating new ideas?"

"I know what works and what doesn't."

The questioning went on like this for a while. Finally Jack asked, "What's the diagnosis?"

"No doubt about it, you're stuck in a rut," the idea doctor proclaimed. "At first I thought it was just a case of plaque-on-the-brain. Then all I'd have to do is prescribe some mental floss. But your situation is more serious."

"That bad, huh?" Jack shrugged.

"Yes. You've got your ends reversed."

"What?"

"You see, the human body has two ends on it—one to create with and one to sit on. As long as you actively pursue new ideas, your creative end stays in good shape. But if you sit around doing the same old things, your brain descends into your rear. The result is that your ends get reversed."

Jack knew that the idea doctor was right. "What causes this?" Jack wanted to know.

The idea doctor replied, "To avoid trying new things, some people develop attitudes about creative thinking that keep them safely stuck where they are. These attitudes are:

It's not important.
I don't have time.
I already have the answer.
I'm not creative.

"They're dangerous because they can cause you to miss some important things. For example, if you're indifferent to creative thinking, then you've failed to see that generating and implementing new ideas are crucial survival skills in a rapidly changing world.

"If you spend your time like a fireman—fighting fires, tending routines, and letting your business manage you rather than the other way around—then you haven't realized that your job might be easier if you engaged in some creative fire prevention.

"If you arrogantly believe that you've already got the right answer, strategy, or approach, you won't find out that there may be a better way to do what you're doing—perhaps until it's too late.

"And if your self-esteem is low, you haven't realized that whether or not you become the next Picasso, Einstein, or Curie, you were born with the ability to probe the world in unique ways, and your challenge is to realize this potential."

Jack listened to this explanation and then he said, "What you've told me makes a lot of sense. I think all these attitudes have influenced my thinking at one time or another during the past year." He then paused for a moment and asked, "Is there any hope? Is there any way to wake up my creative powers?"

"Yes," said the idea doctor. "As a matter of fact, this remedy has been around for centuries."

"Let me have it," Jack said.

At this point, the idea doctor walked up to Jack and gave him a kick in the seat of the pants. Jack was stunned for an instant, but then he jumped up and exclaimed, "I'm going to go out and get some new ideas. I'm going to make something happen." The kick had been just the jolt he needed to get his ends realigned.

"You see, Jack, sometimes nothing short of a kick in the seat of the pants will get people off their duffs to create something new. I'm glad it worked for you."

"Thanks for everything," Jack said as he left.

The Four Roles Of The Creative Process

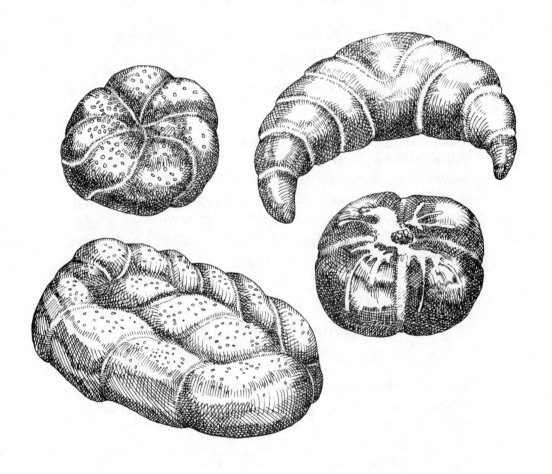

The Four Roles Of The Creative Process

All the world's a stage,
And all the men and women merely players;
They have their entrances and exits;
And one man in his time has many parts.

—William Shakespeare, Playwright

Exercise: What's your creative performance been like lately? (Check the appropriate box.)

☐ High: I generate and apply new ideas every day.

☐ Medium: Occasionally, I'll get a new idea and do something with it.

☐ Low: I'm in real need of a kick in the seat of the pants.

If you're like a lot of people, you probably checked the "medium" box.* Remember, however, that things are changing quickly. What worked last week may not be the best way to solve today's problems or take advantage of next week's opportunities. In such a climate, you need to be constantly coming up with new ideas. So, if you'd like to crank your creativity up a notch (or prevent it from slipping into the "needing a kick" category), you might ask yourself:

What can I do to get my creative performance into high gear?

My advice is to activate the explorer, artist, judge, and warrior within you. To introduce you to this idea, try the following exercise.

---

*If you checked the "high" box, that's great. But remember that even the best lumberjack in the forest has to sharpen his axe occasionally. So keep on reading.

Exercise: Listed below are four questions. If you've done *any* of the activities listed in each question, then check the box next to that question.

1. Have you ever: ☐

- participated in a scavenger hunt?
- looked at a butterfly wing under a microscope or the Crab nebula through a telescope?
- done market research for a new product?
- gone to a conference outside your field?
- asked someone the same question three different ways to find out what they really thought?
- gone camping in a wilderness area?

2. Have you ever: ☐

- cooked a gourmet dinner?
- asked "what if" on a spreadsheet?
- danced at midnight under a full moon?
- written a poem or made up a joke?
- designed an unusual costume for a Halloween party?
- wondered why trees and rivers have similar shapes?

3. Have you ever: ☐

- gone comparison-shopping?
- graded an essay exam?
- made an investment?
- decided to have a baby?
- voted in an election?
- refereed a sporting event?

4. Have you ever: ☐

- made a sales call?
- been involved in competitive sports?
- started a company?
- loved and lost?
- negotiated a contract?
- actively supported a political cause?

We'll get to your answers in just a minute. But first, let's take a look at what this "explorer, artist, judge, and warrior" idea is all about.

During the past few years, I've had an opportunity to work with many creative people: software developers, managers, television producers, comedians, market strategists, journalists, scientists, and designers. Again and again, I've discovered a pattern in how they generate and implement new ideas.

I've found that the hallmark of creative people is their mental flexibility. Like race-car drivers who shift in and out of different gears depending on where they are on the course, creative people are able to shift in and out of different types of thinking depending on the needs of the situation at hand. Sometimes they're open and probing, at others they're playful and off-the-wall. At still other times, they're critical and fault-finding. And finally, they're doggedly persistent in striving to reach their goals. From this, I've concluded that the creative process consists of our adopting four main roles, each of which embodies a different type of thinking. Let's take a closer look. These roles are:

Explorer

Artist

Judge

Warrior

First off, you—as a creative thinker—need the raw materials from which new ideas are made: facts, concepts, experiences, knowledge, feelings, and whatever else you can find. You can look for these in the same old places. However, you're much more likely to find something original if you venture off the beaten path. So, you become an *explorer* and look for the materials you'll use to build your idea. During the course of your searching, you'll poke around in unknown areas, pay attention to unusual patterns, and seek out a variety of different kinds of information.

The ideas you gather will be like so many pieces of colored glass at the end of a kaleidoscope. They may form a pattern, but if you want something new and different, you'll have to give them a twist or two. That's when you shift roles and let the *artist* in you come out. You experiment with a variety of approaches. You follow your intuition. You rearrange things, look at them backwards, and turn them upside down. You ask what-if questions and look for hidden analogies. You may even break the rules or create your own. After all of this you come up with a new idea.

Now you ask yourself, "Is this idea any good? Is it worth pursuing? Will it give me the return I want? Do I have the resources to make this happen?" To help you make your decision, you adopt the mindset of a *judge.* During your evaluation, you critically weigh the evidence. You look for drawbacks in the idea, and wonder if the timing is right. You run risk analyses, question your assumptions, and listen to your gut. Ultimately you make a decision.

Finally it's time to implement your idea. You realize, however, that the world isn't set up to accommodate every new idea that comes along. As a matter of fact, there's a lot of competition out there. If you want your idea to succeed, you'll have to take the offensive. So, you become a *warrior* and take your idea into battle. As a warrior, you're part general and part foot-soldier. You develop your strategy, and commit yourself to reaching your objective. You also have the discipline to slog it out in the trenches. You may have to overcome excuses, idea killers, temporary setbacks, and other obstacles. But you have the courage to do what's necessary to make your idea a reality.

Here, then, is my recommendation for high creative performance:

When you're searching for new information, be an Explorer.

When you're turning your resources into new ideas, be an Artist.

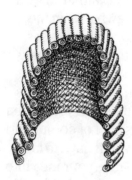

When you're evaluating the merits of an idea, be a Judge.

When you're carrying your idea into action, be a Warrior.

Do you know these creative roles? Sure, everyone has at least some familiarity with them. Refer back to the exercise you took a few moments ago. If you checked box #1, then you know some of the basics of thinking like an explorer. If you checked box #2, then you've got some idea of how to be an artist. If you checked box #3, then you know what it's like to be a judge. And, if you checked box #4, then you've let the warrior in you come out.

Viewed together, these four roles are your creative team for generating and implementing new ideas. Of course, the pattern for most of the things you create won't always be this linear progression of explorer-to-artist-to-judge-to-warrior. Usually there's a fair amount of shifting back and forth between the roles. For example, your judge may return an idea to your artist for further development. Your artist might come up with an idea and tell your explorer to go dig up some information that supports it. Your warrior will tell your judge what's making it in the world and what's not.

In addition, there's no one right way to be creative. Indeed, each creative thinker has his own style. Given a concept to develop or a problem to solve, some people start as the artist and jump back and forth to the explorer and the judge until they reach their objective. Others do it just the reverse. In general, however, you'll be using your explorer more in the early stages of the creative process, your artist and judge more in the middle, and your warrior toward the end.

Exercise: Now, here's a chance for you to rate each of your creative roles.

How would you rate your **Explorer?**

☐ 1. My friends call me "ostrich head."

☐ 2. I see only what's in front of me.

☐ 3. I make time to explore.

☐ 4. "Go and find it" is my middle name.

☐ 5. Columbus, Madame Curie, and Apollo 11 all rolled into one.

How would you rate your **Artist?**

☐ 1. My imagination's in prison.

☐ 2. I can follow a recipe.

☐ 3. I'm usually good for a new insight.

☐ 4. Part magician, part poet, part child.

☐ 5. Picasso and Einstein, make room!

How would you rate your **Judge?**

☐ 1. Decision-making: what's that?

☐ 2. Flipping a coin would get better results.

☐ 3. I can usually pick out what's worth building on in a new idea.

☐ 4. I'm right more often than not.

☐ 5. Wisdom of Solomon.

How would you rate your **Warrior?**

☐ 1. A real wimp.

☐ 2. I'm fine until I hit a good excuse or two.

☐ 3. I get up when I'm knocked down.

☐ 4. I get things done.

☐ 5. In the ranks of Caesar and Patton.

Why are some people bubbling with innovative ideas and others just bumbling along? Let's take a look at two of the main reasons for low creative performance: weak roles and bad timing.

Imagine the consequences of having a weak role in your creative team. If your explorer has his head in the sand, you won't have any new information to draw upon. If your artist's imagination is locked up, you'll end up with run-of-the-mill work that lacks a punch. If your judge's critical faculties are faulty, then you may be saying "yes" to garbage and "no" to potentially good ideas. And if you've got a wimp for a warrior, then you won't be getting many ideas into action. Thus, you have to make a deliberate effort to get and keep all of your roles in good shape. The maxim "use it or lose it" applies as much to creative thinking as it does to any other activity.

Equally important to knowing your creative roles is knowing *when to use them*—timing is paramount. Using a role at the wrong time—such as employing your judge to explore for information or your artist to implement your idea—is counterproductive. It's like driving on the freeway in reverse or trying to back into a parking place in fourth gear. When your timing's off, you won't get much accomplished. Thus, you need to pay attention to the type of thinking required for each situation and then shift into it.

Some people have trouble shifting because they get stuck in a particular role. This can have disastrous results on their creative performance. For example, if you get stuck in your explorer, you may never get around to assembling the information you've gathered into a new idea. If you get stuck in your artist, you may spend all of your time working and re-working your creation and not let go of it. If you get stuck in your judge, you'll inhibit your artist and spend so long evaluating the idea that you'll fail to make a timely decision. And, if you get stuck in your warrior, you'll want to rush everything into action regardless of whether the other roles have done their job or not.

To achieve high performance, develop your creative roles and make sure that you use them at the appropriate time. In this book, we'll take a look at each role and provide some tips and strategies to help you develop it. We'll also have some fun to boot. I hope you get a kick out of it!

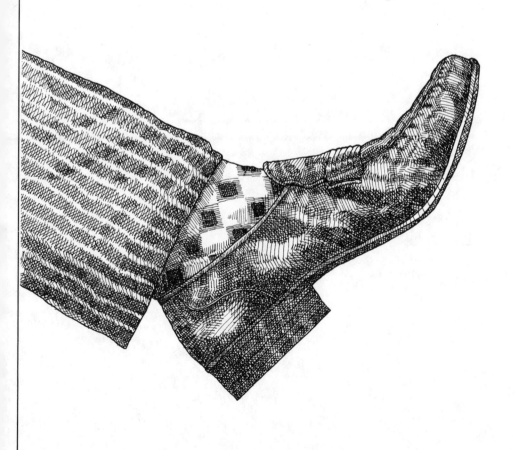

The Explorer

Your role for searching for information

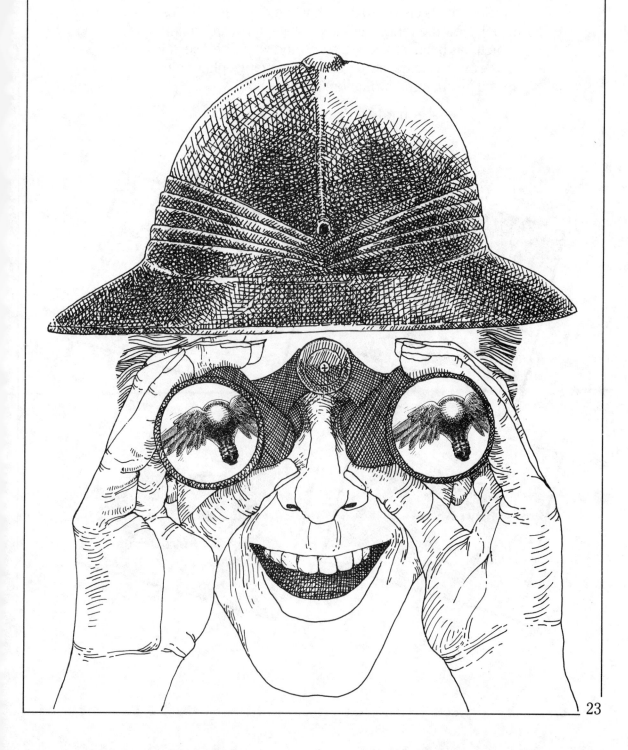

Adopt An Insight Outlook

I roamed the countryside searching for answers to things I did not understand. Why shells existed on the tops of mountains along with the imprints of coral and plants and seaweed usually found in the sea. Why the thunder lasts a longer time than that which causes it and why immediately on its creation the lightning becomes visible to the eye while thunder requires time to travel. How the various circles of water form around the spot which has been struck by a stone and why a bird sustains itself in the air. These questions and other strange phenomena engaged my thought throughout my life.

—Leonardo da Vinci, Renaissance Man

In order to create new ideas, you need the raw materials from which they're made: facts, theories, concepts, rules, information, feelings, and impressions. To help you find them, bring out the first member of your creative team, your explorer.

A good explorer knows that looking for ideas is like prospecting for gold. If you look in the same old places, you'll find tapped-out veins. But if you're curious and poke around in new areas, you'll improve your chances of discovering new idea lodes.

Exploring involves venturing off the beaten path. It also means opening yourself up to the world. Thus, a good explorer has an "insight outlook." That's the attitude that there's a lot of good information available all around you, and all you have to do is find it. With an "insight outlook," you know that in one way or another, the different ideas you find have the potential to come together to form something new. If you go to an airport, you'll find ideas there. If you go to a museum, you'll find ideas there too. And the same applies to hardware stores, garbage dumps, boutiques, libraries, parking garages, wilderness areas, restaurants, botanical gardens, and classrooms. Indeed, the more divergent your sources, the more original the idea you create is likely to be. This chapter contains some of the explorer's basic search strategies.

Know What Your Objective Is

The art of becoming wise is the art of knowing what to overlook.

—William James, Psychologist

I'd rather know some of the questions than all of the answers.

—James Thurber, Humorist

Exercise: Find a perfect star in the pattern below. As you look for it, try to be aware of the search strategies you use.

Life is like a big noisy cocktail party with people talking, glasses clinking, and music playing. But even with all this noise, it's possible for you to understand the person across from you. Or the person twenty feet away. That's because our attention is selective—you can tune in certain things and tune out others.

Take a look around where you're sitting and find five things that have blue in them. Go ahead and do it.

With a "blue" mindset, you'll find that blue jumps right out at you: a blue book on the table, a blue pillow on the couch, blue in the painting on the wall, and so on. Similarly, whenever you learn a new word, you hear it six times in the next two days. In like fashion, you've probably noticed that after you buy a new car, you promptly see that make of car everywhere. (A corollary, one man told me, was when he sold his Buick and stopped seeing Buicks.) That's because people find what they're looking for. If you're looking for conspiracies, you'll find conspiracies. If you're looking for examples of man's good works, you'll find that too. It's all a matter of setting your mental channel.

Let's take a look at the star exercise. How did you do? Did you find it? (Just in case you didn't, try focusing your efforts in the lower right-hand quadrant.) The point of this exercise is that you need to have some idea of what you're looking for in order to find it. So the main question is: did you define what you were looking for? Is it a five-pointed star? A Star of David? A seven-pointed sheriff's star? Is it a big star? A little star? Is it composed of both black and white triangles? An explorer knows that it's important to have thought some of this through before embarking on the search process. As philosopher John Dewey put it, "A problem well-stated is a problem half-solved."

Ask yourself: What am I trying to find?

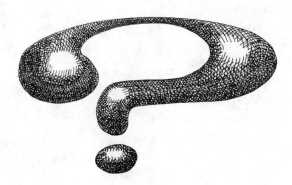

Look In Other Fields

Anyone can look for fashion in a boutique or history in a museum. The creative explorer looks for history in a hardware store and fashion in an airport.

—Robert Wieder, Journalist and Standup-Comedian

Many good ideas have been discovered because someone poked around in an outside industry or discipline, and applied what he found to his own field. Football coach Knute Rockne got the idea for his "four horsemen" backfield shift while watching a burlesque chorus routine. Dan Bricklin took the "spreadsheet" concept from accounting and turned it into VisiCalc, the program that created the microcomputer software industry. World War I military designers borrowed from the cubist art of Picasso and Braque to create more effective camouflage patterns for tanks and guns. Mathematician John von Neumann analyzed poker-table behavior and developed the "game theory" model of economics. The "unbreakable" U.S. military code used in World War II was based on the Navajo language. The Wright brothers were bicycle repairmen. I've known advertising people who got ideas from biology, software programmers who got inspiration from songwriters, and investors who spotted new opportunities by going to junkyards.

It's not surprising that Thomas Edison gave his colleagues this advice: "Make it a practice to keep on the lookout for novel and interesting ideas that others have used successfully. Your idea has to be original only in its adaptation to the problem you are working on."

Exercise: Bionics is a field of engineering in which ideas from natural systems are "borrowed" and adapted for human uses. Listed below are some examples of this. See if you can connect each specimen with its subsequent engineering application.

Specimen	Engineering Application
1. Elm tree seeds: "wing structure"	A. Device for detecting poisonous mine gases
2. Fly: vertical takeoff	B. Infrared photography
3. Salmon: organ for detecting extremely dilute solutions of odoriferous liquid	C. Improved windmill design; safer helicopters; improved ski design
4. Burdock burr: hooked spines	D. Fiberglass-reinforced plastics
5. Moth: antenna is olfactory organ of high sensitivity	E. Improved hydrophone design
6. Snake: thermoscopic vision that detects 0.002° C. temp. gradient	F. Reliable celestial compass
7. Bamboo stalk: two-phase composite fiber construction	G. Device for detecting pollutants in water
8. Beehive: hexagonal construction	H. Vertical take-off aircraft
9. Bee eyes: segment facets filter polarized light	I. Basis for a commercial fastener
10. Seals: hearing apparatus for underwater sound detection	J. Stronger and lighter pool tables

Tip: There may be gem of an idea lying in the field next to yours. Cross the border and take a look.

Look For Lots Of Ideas

Nothing is more dangerous than an idea when it is the only one you have.

—Émile Chartier, Philosopher

Exercise: What is this a picture of?

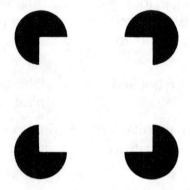

When two-time Nobel Prize winner Linus Pauling said, "The best way to get a good idea is to get a lot of ideas," he was describing the low-probability nature of creative thinking. The odds that any particular idea will help solve your problem aren't that high. But the more you get, the closer you are to reaching your objective. Thus, it's important to get as many "right answers" as you can. You may not be able to use all of them later on, but that's for your judge to decide—not a constraint that should limit your explorer. Thus, your explorer has the attitude that everything has some value; nothing is worthless.

This is why a professional photographer takes so many pictures when shooting an important subject. He may take thirty, fifty, a hundred or more shots. He'll change the exposure, the lighting, the filters, and so on. That's because he knows that out of all of the pictures he takes, a few of them will be good. One photographer told me that he went on a whaling expedition and took over 850 shots. Out of these only eleven were "good" enough to show his friends.

Computer scientist Alan Kay (the man who coined the term "personal computer") believes in the value of looking for lots of ideas.

> If you take the smartest people you know and give them a glass of wine so that they'll really level with you, they'll tell you that nineteen out of every twenty ideas they have aren't any good. But it's because they generate so many ideas that they're able to come up with a few exceptional ones.

Inventor Ray Dolby (the man who took the "hiss" out of recorded music) has a similar philosophy. He says:

> Inventing is a skill that some people have and some people don't. But you can learn how to invent. You have to have the will not to jump at the first solution ... because the really elegant solution might be right around the corner. The most likely inventor candidate would be someone who says, "Yes, that's one way to do it, but it doesn't seem to be an optimum solution." Then he keeps on thinking.

When you look for more than one right answer, you allow your imagination to open up. What does the figure you just saw look like? It looks like a square. What else? How about four hungry circles? Tag-team Pac-man? Mickey Mouse looking in a mirror? What else?

How do you keep a fish from smelling? Cook it as soon as you catch it. Freeze it. Wrap it in paper. Keep a cat around. Burn incense. Leave it in the water. Cut its nose off.

Tip: Look beyond the first right answer.

One Thing Can Lead To
Something Completely Different

If you do not expect the unexpected you will not find it, for it is not to be reached by search or trail.

—Heraclitus, Philosopher

Alexander Graham Bell was trying to invent a hearing aid. Columbus was looking for India. Colonel Sanders set out to sell his chicken recipe to restaurants. Physicist Karl Jansky improvised a new antenna to study the effects of telephone static. Instead, he discovered radio waves from the Milky Way, and in the process helped to create the science of radio astronomy. Often what we're looking for leads us to something much different. Thus, it's important for the explorer to be willing to be led astray. It's for the judge to keep the "practical" in mind—not the explorer.

I once asked Apple Computer co-founder Steve Jobs why some people are more creative than others. He replied, "Innovation is usually the result of connections of past experiences— and luck. But if you have the same experiences as everybody else, you're unlikely to look in a different direction. For example, I went to Reed College in Portland. At Reed, most of the men took modern dance classes from a woman named Judy Massey. We did it to meet the women. I didn't realize how much I had learned about movement and perception from that class until a few years later when I worked for Nolan Bushnell at Atari. I was able to relate how much resolution of movement you need in terms of perceiving things in certain ways for video games." Jobs was trying to get a date; instead he ended up fine-tuning the video game *Breakout.* (This probably got him a lot of dates.)

Think about the times in your own life where one thing has led to something different. How did you get interested in your line of work? How did you meet your spouse? Think of the times you've gone to the library in search of a particular book, and then found something even better and juicier on the shelf behind you. As writer Franklin Adams put it, "I find that a great part of the information I have was acquired by looking up something and finding something else on the way."

Tip: Expect the unexpected. Open your mind up to things that have no connection with the problem you're trying to solve. This may lead to the information that makes the big difference in the development of your idea. Here are some things you might do: subscribe to an unusual magazine—perhaps one from the opposite political point of view. Spend a morning at an elementary school or an afternoon at a senior citizen center. Go to work two hours early. Scrape together a small amount of money and buy a share of stock in companies from three different industries. Test drive an exotic car. Attend a city council meeting. Dig out some old magazines from the 1940's and 1950's. Try an Indonesian recipe. Spend a day in another city. Study ancient history.

Shift Your Focus

Exercise: I've divided the first ten letters of the alphabet into two groups.

Group #1 is: A E F H I

Group #2 is: B C D G J

What is the pattern that differentiates the two groups? If you recognize it, which group would you put *K* into? How about *R?* Or *T?*

I think much of what we call "intelligence" is our ability to recognize patterns. We recognize similarities (stellar galaxies and water emptying from a bathtub spiral in the same way), sequences (the steps you go through to start a car), processes (how to convert grapes into wine), cycles (the periodic boom and bust of the pork belly market), distributions (the large number of post World War II babies), movements (smoke over an airplane wing in a wind tunnel), shapes (cracks in dried mud usually form 120° angles), tendencies (the influence of anyone who appears on the cover of *Time* magazine has crested), and probabilities (the 49ers usually win their home games).

To solve the above alphabet problem, you had to figure out what sort of pattern I had in mind when I determined whether a letter belonged in Group #1 or Group #2. Some people look at this problem and try to figure out some sort of logical progression. If, however, you look for a different type of pattern and focus not on the sequence in which the information is given, but on its shape, you might notice that the letters in Group #1 have only straight lines, while the letters in Group #2 have both straight and curved lines. Thus, *K* and *T* would fit into Group #1 while *R* belongs in Group #2.

Tip: Pay attention to different kinds of information. You just may come up with a pattern you wouldn't have discovered otherwise. If you're logically oriented, focus on how something feels. If you're visually oriented, focus on the "smell" of a situation. Indeed, a fun exercise is to construct an "olfactory map" of the various smells in your world. Here's a start: what are three things you smell right now? Do you notice a pattern?

Don't Overlook The Obvious

Sometimes the most helpful ideas are right in front of us. As the noted explorer Scott Love once put it, "Only the most foolish of mice would hide in a cat's ear. But only the wisest of cats would think to look there."

Here's a good example of people missing the obvious. If you study the evolution of the bicycle during the 1860's and 1870's, you'll notice that both wheels start out at about the same size, but over time the front wheel gets larger and larger, and the rear wheel becomes significantly smaller. The reason was that initially the pedals were attached directly to the front wheel. Since there was no drive train (no one had thought of it), the only way to get the bike to go faster was to make the front wheel bigger. The culmination of this trend was the "penny-farthing" model with a front wheel almost five feet (1.5 m.) in diameter. Needless to say, they weren't very safe.

The curious thing about this whole development is that the solution for a better and safer bicycle was right in front of bicycle inventors.   The bicycles themselves were manufactured using drive chain technology! Finally, someone looked up, made the obvious connection, and asked "Why not use the drive chain to power the rear wheel?" H.J. Lawson was the first to construct such a model, and within only a few years this safer model supplanted the penny farthing.

Ask yourself: What resources are right in front of me?

Pay Attention To The Small Things

Small things can have a big impact—especially when combined and leveraged with other things. For example, a small change anywhere in the world's weather system can have enormous ramifications. In the winter of 1982–83, all the Pacific weather patterns got out of whack. The result: deadly droughts scorched India, Indonesia, and Australia while the west coast of North America was battered by violent storms, record rains, and high tides. For months meteorologists were baffled as to the cause of these weather changes. Finally, they realized that an *El Niño*—a slight warming of the ocean off of Ecuador—had uncharacteristically spread west and caused these changes throughout the Pacific. When *El Niño* went away, the weather patterns returned to normal.

Why are today's competitive swimmers significantly faster compared to those of twenty years ago? Are they bigger? Better fed? Do their coaches have a better understanding of stroke technique? These are all important reasons, but one small thing that's had a huge impact on swimming is the development of the lightweight binocular swimming goggle. Since swimmers work out in chlorinated water, a typical swimmer without goggles can only go 2,000–3,000 meters per session without eye irritation. The invention of the lightweight goggle protected swimmers' eyes so they could work out for longer and longer distances. In fact, 15,000 to 20,000 meters a day isn't uncommon for Olympic swimmers in training. With such conditioning, it's no wonder times have come down so much.

Ask yourself: What are some small things that could have a big impact on the development of my idea?

Look At The Big Picture

My advice to any young person at the beginning of their career is to try to look for the mere outlines of big things with their fresh, untrained, and unprejudiced mind.

—Hans Selye, Physician

It's easy to get so immersed in the trees of a problem that you fail to see the forest. A good explorer knows that it's important to stand back occasionally and take a look at the larger implications of what he's doing.

One day in the late 1860's, an Iowa farmer left his fields for an hour to watch the construction of the transcontinental railroad near his farm. He watched the track being laid. A few minutes later a steam locomotive came through. The farmer went back to his fields and thought, "So that's what railroading is all about: tracks and trains." What didn't the farmer see about the railroad's possibilities? He didn't see that he could get his products to market much more quickly, that he could get them to many new markets, and that once there they would have to compete against products from many more places. He didn't see the rise of Chicago, Kansas City, Denver, and San Francisco, and the development of intercontinental trade. He didn't see that it would be possible to go across country in less than a week, and that people's perspective on distance and time would change. He didn't see that more opinions and ideas would be shared, and that more and different people would meet, fall in love, and get married. He saw the steel tracks and the locomotive, but he didn't see the consequences.

In the 1930's, France constructed the Maginot Line—a series of fortifications on its northeastern border with Germany—to prevent a quick attack on vital industries. Throughout this period, the French Parliament commissioned several high level panels to study reports that contractors had over-charged the government in building the bunkers. These panels did their job well except for one thing. They didn't stand back to ask the larger question about the strategic utility of the Maginot Line, which was, "Is it militarily correct in light of the advances being made in mechanized warfare?" Had they asked this, they would have come to the same conclusion the Germans did. The latter easily circumvented the Maginot Line and occupied France in 1940.

In the early 1950's, business machine manufacturers thought that the market for computers was small because there were only a half dozen companies and government agencies that needed the computer's enormous number-crunching capability. Only when they stopped looking at computers as pieces of hardware, and started thinking about them as tools for "moving and transforming information" did they discover the enormous potential market for their products.

Ask yourself: What are the major implications of my idea?

Slay A Dragon

Where are the places you're afraid to look for ideas? Centuries ago, when map makers ran out of known world before they ran out of parchment, they would sketch a dragon at the edge of the scroll. This was a sign to the explorer that he would be entering unknown territory at his own risk. Unfortunately, some explorers took this symbol literally and were afraid to push on to new worlds. Other more adventuresome explorers saw the dragons as a sign of opportunity, a door to virgin territory.

Each of us has a mental map of the world in our heads that contains the information we use to guide ourselves in our day-to-day encounters. Like the maps of long ago, our mental maps also have dragons on them. These represent things that, for whatever reason, we don't want to do or push beyond. It could be a fear of public speaking. It could be a fear of going to a party where you don't know any of the people. It could be a desire not to participate in a particular sport. Sometimes these dragons are valid. Sometimes, however, they prevent your explorer from discovering new information.

Ask yourself:
Where do I see dragons? Are they a sign of danger or opportunity? And, if it's the latter, shouldn't I be taking a look? Slay a dragon today.

Use Obstacles To Break Out Of Ruts

Let's suppose that you have a routine. It could be the way you drive to work, cook dinner, or manage a project. Now let's suppose that one day you get half way through this routine and find an obstacle blocking your path. How do you deal with it? You could try to knock it over or remove it. You might return to your starting point, or question your motives.

Another approach is to get off the path and look for an alternative way to your objective. While looking, you may only find a longer way to your objective. But there's the chance that when you're out there searching, you might find something even better than you were initially looking for, and you wouldn't have found it had you not been knocked off the path.

For many years the routine way to finance the purchase of a home was the 30-year fixed-interest mortgage. When the cost of money went over 20% in the late 1970's, however, this method was no longer possible for most home buyers and sellers. As a result of being "knocked off the path," they were forced to look for alternatives, and they discovered such financing vehicles as RRM's (renegotiated rate mortgages), SAM's (shared appreciation mortgages), wraparounds, bartering, trading, and assumable loans.

Not long ago, the pool where my Masters swimming team works out was closed for a month of maintenance. During the downtime, the members had to practice with various other clubs in the area. When we were re-united a month later, there was a great outpouring of new workout ideas. One person had been with a team that had low rest-interval workouts, and she shared those. Another person came back with a heartbeat interval workout. Another discovered a new type of ankle pull-buoy. All of these ideas were discovered because we were forced to break our routine.

Tip: Try programming "interruptions" into your routine. Change your working hours. Take a different way to work. Listen to different radio stations. Cultivate new and different friends. Try a different recipe.

Find The Ideas You Already Have

Imagine that you're sitting in the middle of a dark attic filled with various objects, devices, albums, and books. You have a small flashlight with you. You turn it on and point it in one direction illuminating a picture of you at your senior prom. Your mind conjures up all kinds of images associated with party dresses, staying up late, and fast car rides. Next you swing the light around and stop at a compass. Now you begin to think of navigating your way through a wilderness area. You focus the light on another object, this time a nutcracker and now you think of Christmas.

Your mind is like a dark attic cluttered with experiences and ideas. You don't think about these most of the time because your small light of consciousness isn't shining on them. But if you had a way of forcing your light around the room, you might discover more of what you have.

A good way to turn your mental attic of experiences into a treasure room is to use "trigger concepts" —words that will spark a fresh association of ideas in your mind. Like pebbles dropping in a pond, they stimulate other associations, some of which may help you find something new. A list of potential triggers is given in Table I.

Table I: Trigger Concepts

	1	2	3	4	5	6	7	8	9	10
001-010	Skeleton	Room	Treadmill	Oven	Filter	Root	Temple	Window	Star	Typewriter
011-020	Valley	Fruit	Library	Purse	Molecule	Battery	Armor	Fountain	Bed	Seed
021-030	Maze	Water	Air	Earth	Money	Spice	Bell	Rock	Album	Robot
031-040	Tunnel	Altar	Diamond	Army	Computer	Bag	Tide	Bank	Weapon	Farm
041-050	Amoeba	Anvil	Bait	Balloon	Bible	Hinge	Horse	Image	Junk	Knot
051-060	Algebra	Alphabet	Child	Lamp	Leg	Liquid	Manual	Match	Sex	Data Base
061-070	Menu	Prison	Monster	Muscle	Nest	Nut	Opium	Page	Parasite	Pendulum
071-080	Pepper	Pill	Satellite	Pod	Ring	Port	Prism	Puzzle	Radio	Microscope
081-090	Rainbow	Rudder	Safe	Sauce	Saloon	Shadow	Shovel	Smoke	Rash	Horizon
091-100	Ice	Index	Key	Ladder	Landslide	Lever	Lock	Machine	Map	Mattress
101-110	Meteor	Mist	Moon	Music	Net	Ocean	Sphere	Paint	Passport	Perfume
111-120	Perfume	Pipe	Plant	Pond	Pore	Prison	Pyramid	Raft	Record	River
121-130	Rope	Rug	Sand	Saw	Screw	Shell	Signature	Herb	Hose	Icon
131-140	Insect	Kitchen	Ladle	Leaf	Library	Lode	Magnet	Marsh	Meat	Horoscope
141-150	Nail	Meter	Missile	Motor	Organ	Nose	Onion	Palette	Pebble	Star
151-160	Vise	Pillow	Plate	Pool	Stamp	Pulley	Quilt	Rag	Ramp	Rifle
161-170	Robot	Rose	Sandwich	Ruler	Scale	Script	Shoe	Siren	House	Hieroglyph
171-180	Vulture	Joint	Kite	Lake	Lens	Milk	Loom	Mask	Medal	Lightning
181-190	Mountain	Needle	Vertebra	Violin	Pacemaker	Soap	Pen	Knife	Piano	Planet
191-200	Pocket	Dung	Powder	Pump	Radar	Rain	Halo	Rubber	Saddle	Parachute
201-210	Cup	School	Program	Ship	Skin	Zone	Road	Ball	Zoo	Trigger
211-220	Umbrella	Channel	Crystal	Woman	Man	Caldron	Cannon	Chain	Chord	Cloud
221-230	Copy	Cycle	Plow	Egg	Hook	Drain	Drum	Tree	Bomb	Wing
231-240	Well	Water	Treasure	Flag	Guitar	Flood	Fog	Fork	Fungus	Furniture
241-250	Girdle	Glue	Hair	Template	Harbor	Mirror	Camera	Wedge	Wave	Sandpaper
251-260	Bridge	Network	Staircase	Cave	Food	Cinema	Clock	Crown	Desert	Chessboard
261-270	Water	Dust	Eraser	Statue	Net	Parachute	Gate	Pump	Broom	Bottleneck
271-280	Antenna	Floor	Flower	Food	Block	Fossil	Funhouse	Gate	Glacier	Ratchet Wheel
281-290	God	Guillotine	Bee	Plug	Blanket	Funnel	Book	Brain	Brakes	Booby Trap
291-300	Trap	Tube	Spring	Television	Toilet	Buffer	Weed	Cancer	Cell	Cesspool
301-310	Compass	Circle	Code	Web	Dress	Current	Detour	Ear	Button	Face
311-320	Factory	Fairy	Fan	Farm	Feather	Fertilizer	Field	Finger	Engine	Floodlight
321-330	Foam	Fly	Foot	Bird	Bottle	Hole	Color	Dope	Adult	Forge
331-340	Game	Garden	Gear	Ghost	Glass	Graph	Gun	Gutter	Bruise	Bug
341-350	Circus	Hammer	Head	Heart	Family	Blister	Acid	Candy	Chorus	Springboard
351-360	Die	Body	Drill	Eye	Family	Fish	Fence	Festival	Film	Fire
361-370	Spotlight	Frame	Glove	Hand	Song	Grave	Lever	Sphere	Square	Sun
371-380	Table	Tool	Trail	Vent	Vegetable	Soup	Spiral	Shaft	Market	Torpedo
381-390	Target	Telescope	Weirdness	Sword	Torch	Train	Triangle	Vacuum	Ticket	Thermometer
391-400	Spear	Sponge	Stomach	Memory	Spectrum	Telephone	Stove	Tapestry	Car	Kaleidoscope

Table II: Random Numbers 1–400

268 107 064 316 127 205 335 239 037 104 338 214 155 096 011 125 216 238 324 318 042 078 134 168 196 212 246 241 361 353 261 192 066 081 301 397 343

273 147 121 283 100 247 391 067 204 363 094 135 189 143 172 077 244 163 373 398 259 102 015 298 365 063 291 092 190 384 091 009 368 342 295 087 106

003 208 317 306 293 165 356 386 381 017 350 174 394 073 082 103 053 019 024 367 182 038 319 114 132 173 284 375 022 133 083 357 390 183 282 233 256

160 341 371 392 080 232 289 098 093 349 029 206 116 090 333 162 138 345 272 178 071 034 191 360 399 311 257 382 200 331 245 234 052 197 315 139 141

144 337 281 112 023 326 177 150 152 254 164 299 385 400 253 277 366 027 328 020 278 307 065 325 145 266 084 262 290 252 313 288 310 222 167 215 393

312 279 379 260 058 270 005 153 171 358 370 332 040 105 217 396 056 201 314 250 355 322 237 117 195 225 224 235 377 158 240 068 036 130 043 210 010

286 089 026 045 271 025 124 226 184 364 378 354 049 012 044 287 146 166 021 255 383 007 120 320 075 057 264 142 101 251 119 292 374 006 123 387 181

018 265 352 137 207 303 347 050 110 263 218 193 109 061 380 097 169 186 001 060 035 213 062 269 389 249 047 376 115 294 220 140 179 113 039 126 074

236 359 348 296 344 228 088 229 032 300 170 014 221 076 243 069 185 149 154 046 041 388 199 180 329 030 198 028 227 194 276 161 297 372 079 033 336

070 151 118 309 031 285 159 013 334 072 267 369 099 055 302 051 148 203 209 187 323 085 008 362 095 054 339 346 330 059 108 136 327 157 304 242 131

129 004 122 395 248 274 219 016 340 280 111 156 188 176 175 321 258 086 128 002 351 275 308 230 223 305 231 211 048 202 184 364 378 354 049 012 044

287 146 166 021 255 383 007 120 320 075 057 264 142 243 069 185 149 154 046 041 388 199 180 329 030 198 028 227 194 276 161 297 372 298 365 063 291

092 190 384 091 009 368 342 295 087 106 003 208 317 306 293 165 270 005 153 171 358 370 332 040 105 217 396 056 201 314 250 355 322 237 117 195 225

224 235 377 158 240 068 036 130 043 178 071 034 191 360 399 311 257 382 200 331 245 234 052 197 315 139 141 144 337 281 112 023 326 177 150 152 254

164 299 385 400 253 277 366 027 328 020 278 307 053 019 024 367 182 038 319 114 132 173 284 375 022 133 083 357 390 183 282 233 256 160 341 371 392

080 232 289 098 093 356 386 381 017 350 174 394 073 082 103 213 062 269 389 249 047 376 115 294 220 079 033 336 070 151 118 309 031 285 159 338 214

155 096 011 125 216 238 324 318 042 078 134 168 196 212 246 241 361 353 013 334 072 267 369 099 055 302 051 148 203 209 187 323 085 008 362 095 054

339 346 330 059 108 136 327 157 304 242 131 065 325 145 266 084 262 290 252 313 288 210 010 286 089 026 045 271 025 124 226 129 004 122 395 248 274

219 016 340 280 111 156 188 176 175 321 258 086 128 002 310 222 167 215 393 312 279 379 260 058 268 107 064 316 127 205 335 239 037 104 261 192 066

081 301 397 343 273 147 121 283 100 247 391 067 204 363 094 135 189 143 172 077 244 163 373 398 259 102 015 349 029 206 116 090 333 162 138 345 272

101 251 119 292 374 006 123 387 181 018 351 275 308 230 223 305 231 211 048 202 140 179 113 039 126 074 236 359 348 296 344 228 088 229 032 300 170

014 221 076 265 352 137 207 303 347 050 110 263 218 193 109 061 380 097 169 186 001 060 035 268 107 064 316 127 205 335 239 037 104 338 214 155 096

011 125 216 238 324 318 042 078 134 168 196 212 246 241 361 353 261 192 066 081 301 397 343 273 147 121 283 100 247 391 067 204 363 094 135 189 143

172 077 244 163 373 398 259 102 015 298 365 063 291 092 190 384 091 009 368 342 295 087 106 003 208 317 306 293 165 356 386 381 017 350 174 394 073

082 103 053 019 024 367 182 038 319 114 132 173 284 375 022 133 083 357 390 183 282 233 256 160 341 371 392 080 232 289 098 093 349 029 206 116 090

333 162 138 345 272 178 071 034 191 360 399 311 257 382 200 331 245 234 052 197 315 139 141 144 337 281 112 023 326 177 150 152 254 164 299 385 400

253 277 366 027 328 020 278 307 065 325 145 266 084 262 290 252 313 288 310 222 167 215 393 312 279 379 260 058 270 005 153 171 358 370 332 040 105

217 396 056 201 314 250 355 322 237 117 195 225 224 235 377 158 240 068 036 130 043 210 010 286 089 026 045 271 025 124 226 184 364 378 354 049 012

044 287 146 166 021 255 383 007 120 320 075 057 264 142 101 251 119 292 374 006 123 387 181 018 265 352 137 207 303 347 050 110 263 218 193 109 061

380 097 169 186 001 060 035 213 062 269 389 249 047 376 115 294 220 140 179 113 039 126 074 236 359 348 296 344 228 088 229 032 300 170 014 221 076

243 069 185 149 154 046 041 388 199 180 329 030 198 028 227 194 276 161 297 372 079 033 336 070 151 118 309 031 285 159 013 334 072 267 369 099 055

302 051 148 203 209 187 323 085 008 362 095 054 339 346 330 059 108 136 327 157 304 242 131 129 004 122 395 248 274 219 016 340 280 111 156 188 176

175 321 258 086 128 002 351 275 308 230 223 305 231 211 048 202 184 364 378 354 049 012 044 287 146 166 021 255 383 007 120 320 075 057 264 142 243

069 185 149 154 046 041 388 199 180 329 030 198 028 227 194 276 161 297 372 298 365 063 291 092 190 384 091 009 368 342 295 087 106 003 208 317 306

293 165 270 005 153 171 358 370 332 040 105 217 396 056 201 314 250 355 322 237 117 195 225 224 235 377 158 240 068 036 130 043 178 071 034 191 360

399 311 257 382 200 331 245 234 052 197 315 139 141 144 337 281 112 023 326 177 150 152 254 164 299 385 400 253 277 366 027 328 020 278 307 053 019

024 367 182 038 319 114 132 173 284 375 022 133 083 357 390 183 282 233 256 160 341 371 392 080 232 289 098 093 356 386 381 017 350 174 394 073 082

103 213 062 269 389 249 047 376 115 294 220 079 033 336 070 151 118 309 031 285 159 338 214 155 096 011 125 216 238 324 318 042 078 134 168 196 212

246 241 361 353 013 334 072 267 369 099 055 302 051 148 203 209 187 323 085 008 362 095 054 339 346 330 059 108 136 327 157 304 242 131 065 325 145

266 084 262 290 252 313 288 210 010 286 089 026 045 271 025 124 226 129 004 122 395 248 274 219 016 340 280 111 156 188 176 175 321 258 086 128 002

310 222 167 215 393 312 279 379 260 058 268 107 064 316 127 205 335 239 037 104 261 192 066 081 301 397 343 273 147 121 283 100 247 391 067 204 363

094 135 189 143 172 077 244 163 373 398 259 102 015 349 029 206 116 090 333 162 138 345 272 101 251 119 292 374 006 123 387 181 018 351 275 308 230

223 305 231 211 048 202 140 179 113 039 126 074 236 359 348 296 344 228 088 229 032 300 170 014 221 076 265 352 137 207 303 347 050 110 263 218 193

109 061 380 097 169 186 001 060 035 385 400 253 277 366 027 328 020 278 307 065 325 145 266 084 262 290 252 313 288 310 222 167 215 393 312 279 379

260 058 270 005 153 171 358 370 332 040 105 217 396 056 201 314 250 355 322 237 117 195 225 224 235 377 158 240 068 036 130 043 210 010 286 089 026

045 271 025 124 226 184 364 378 354 049 012 044 287 146 166 021 255 383 007 120 320 075 057 264 142 101 251 119 292 374 006 123 387 181 018 265 352

137 207 303 347 050 110 263 218 193 109 061 380 097 169 186 001 060 035 213 062 269 389 249 047 376 115 294 220 140 179 113 039 126 074 236 359 348

296 344 228 088 229 032 300 170 014 221 076 243 069 185 149 154 046 041 388 199 180 329 030 198 028 227 194 276 161 297 372 079 033 336 070 151 118

309 031 285 159 013 334 072 267 369 099 055 302 051 148 203 209 187 323 085 008 362 095 054 339 346 330 059 108 136 327 157 304 242 131 129 004 122

395 248 274 219 016 340 280 111 156 188 176 175 321 258 086 128 002 351 275 308 230 223 305 231 211 048 202 184 364 378 354 049 012 044 287 146 166

021 255 383 007 120 320 075 057 264 142 243 069 185 149 154 046 041 388 199 180 329 030 198 028 227 194 276 161 297 372 298 365 063 291 092 190 384

091 009 368 342 295 087 106 003 208 317 306 293 165 270 005 153 171 358 370 332 040 105 217 396 056 201 314 250 355 322 237 117 195 225 224 235 377

I've chosen these for several reasons. First, you already know them; they're simple objects that you've assimilated into your thinking. Second, they're all visual; you can already see each of them in your mind. This is quite important; much of creative thinking is visual in orientation. Indeed, a study of one hundred leading mathematicians showed that they did their best work when they had images in their minds, not when they were thinking of mathematical symbols. Third, and most important, these concepts are "link-rich," that is, it's easy to think of other ideas that are similar or in some way linked to them. For example, "pocket" might trigger you to think of pants, jackets, shirts, pool tables, pita bread, bags, and jars.

There are several ways to select a trigger concept. One is to look through the list until you find one you like. Another is to close your eyes and put your finger on the page. A third way is to use the random numbers listed in Table II. Put your finger on one of the numbers and then find the corresponding trigger concept. If your finger stops at "137," your concept is "magnet."

Now think of things associated with your concept. For example, what does a magnet do? It attracts. What are things that attract? What are some other magnets? Good land is a magnet for developers. Beer is a magnet for slugs. A weak cornerback is a magnet for passes in his area. A rock star is a magnet for groupies. A state with low taxes is a magnet for new business. Other associations might be based on things you might find located nearby your concept. If your trigger concept were "shoe," nearby things could be sock, floor, polish, galoshes, rug, foot odor, athlete's foot, staircases, ankle bracelets, dancing, etc.

How do you use trigger concepts to generate ideas? One way to use them is to make a forced connection between one of the trigger concepts and a problem or idea you'd like to get a different slant on. For example, as I write this, I'm looking for ideas. I draw the trigger concept "hook," and start thinking about "hooks." Does this book have a hook at the beginning to draw the reader in, to get his or her attention? Are there hooks all the way through? A hook is sometimes a barb. Are there any (un)intentional barbs in it? In vaudeville a hook was used to pull the bad acts off the stage. How can I prevent that? What are other things that have hooks? A cane is shaped like a hook. Can I make this book palatable to an older audience? Candy canes have a hook. Can I finish it in time for Christmas?

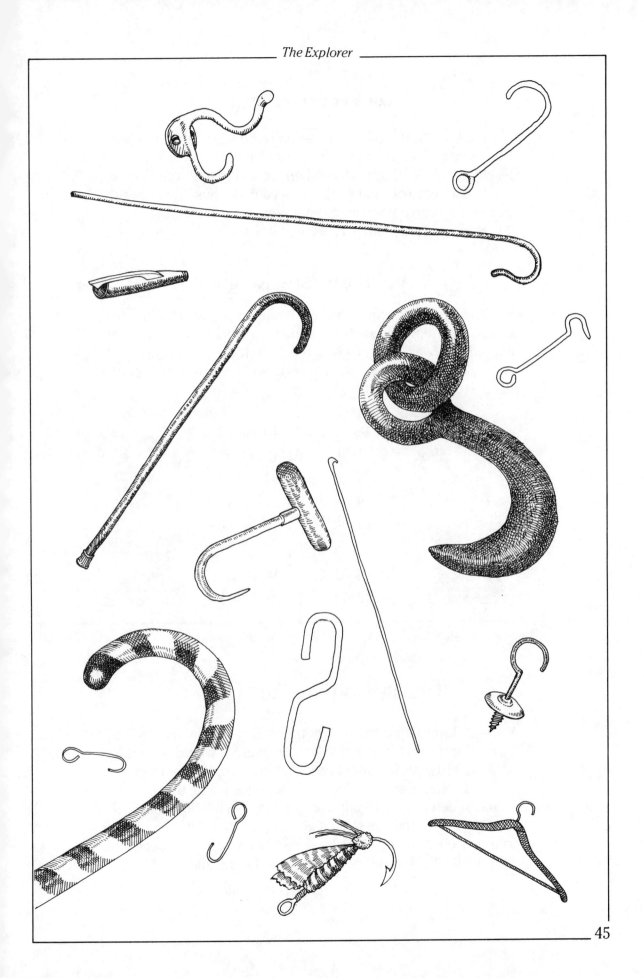

Look For Fun Things

Look for things that you personally think are fun, and keep a file of them. It could be quote, an unusual pattern, or a law describing life. Perhaps, somewhere down the road you may be able to use some of what you've collected. Because these things are fun, they can help to make your idea more interesting.

Here are some things I have in my "fun file."

A Square For A Knight

The eighteenth century mathematician Leonhard Euler made a square where each horizontal or vertical row totals 260; stopping halfway on each gives 130. Even more intriguing is that a chess knight, starting its L-shaped moves from square 1, can hit all 64 squares in numerical order.

1	48	31	50	33	16	63	18
30	51	46	3	62	19	14	35
47	2	49	32	15	34	17	64
52	29	4	45	20	61	36	13
5	44	25	56	9	40	21	60
28	53	8	41	24	57	12	37
43	6	55	26	39	10	59	22
54	27	42	7	58	23	38	11

Gravity Doubled And Halved

Were the force of gravity to be doubled, our bipedal form would be a failure. The majority of terrestrial animals would resemble snakes. Birds would suffer likewise. But, insects would suffer less and some of the smaller would hardly change; microbes would undergo no hardships nor change. On the other hand, if gravity were halved, we should get a lighter, slender, more active form, need less energy, less heat, less lungs, and less blood and muscle. But the microbes would not profit one bit.

—D'Arcy Thompson, Morphologist

Squashed Eggs

When Columbus was at the Royal court in Spain, he asked the courtiers if they could get an egg to stand on end. They tried and tried but couldn't get it stand upright. He then boiled the egg and squashed it down. They said, "That's not fair, you broke the rules." He replied, "Everything is fair once you've done it."

Strawberry Shortcake For 25,000 People

Ever wonder why large projects usually run into unforeseen problems, delays, and headaches? Here's one explanation. Let's suppose that you have a recipe for strawberry shortcake that serves four people. One day you invite over seven friends to eat this dessert. To make it, you simply double the recipe's proportions. On another occasion, you invite over one friend for this dessert. To make it, all you have to do is halve the proportions in the recipe. Now, let's suppose that you invite 25,000 of your closest friends over for strawberry shortcake. Now, the most difficult parts of the problem are no longer given in the recipe. These things include doing futures buying of strawberries on the commodities market; making deals with the Teamsters to deliver enough cream; large scale renting of bowls, spoons, tables, and chairs; and traffic flow coordination. The same thing happens in large projects: things come up that weren't even thought about in the original plans.

—Jack Grimes, Philosopher
(adapted from Bob Barton, Computer Architect)

Three Propositions

1. Software engineering is like looking for a black cat in a dark room.

2. Systems engineering is like looking for a black cat in a dark room in which there is no cat.

3. Knowledge engineering is like looking for a black cat in a dark room where there is no cat and someone yells, "I got it!"

—From a bulletin board at Syntelligence Corporation,
quoted by Brock Brower

Joe Eddy Brown's Paper Airplane

B

C

A

Fly this-a-way ⟶

Here's how to make Joe Eddy Brown's favorite paper airplane. First off, photocopy this page. Then cut out rectangles A, B, and C. Then make A and B into loops and glue (or tape) them to the ends of a folded-up C. Now fly it. Try experimenting with various lengths.

← C ↗

B

A

Big Al Juodikis's Rules Of Life

❊ If Jack's in love, he's no judge of Jill's beauty.

❊ Too much of the world is run on the theory that you don't need road manners if you are a five-ton truck.

❊ It is difficult to see the picture when you are inside the frame.

❊ One meets his destiny often in the road he takes to avoid it.

❊ When it comes to helping you, some people stop at nothing.

❊ After learning the tricks of the trade, many of us think we know the trade.

❊ One of these days is none of these days.

❊ We hear and apprehend only what we already know.

❊ Life is like playing a violin solo and learning the instrument as one goes on.

❊ The dog that trots about finds a bone.

❊ The man who waits for things to turn up has his eyes on his toes.

Tom Hirshfield's Rules of Thumb

✤ If you hit every time the target's too near.

✤ Never learn details before deciding on a first approach.

✤ Never state a problem to yourself in the same terms as it was brought to you.

✤ The second assault on the same problem should come from a totally different direction.

✤ If you don't understand a problem, then explain it to an audience and listen to yourself.

✤ Don't mind approaches that transform one problem into another, that's a new chance.

✤ If it's surprising it's useful.

✤ Studying the inverse problem always helps.

✤ Spend a proportion of your time analyzing your work methods.

Write It Down

A new discovery, a new idea, a new piece of information can come at any time. When it does, be ready to record it. Before I started this practice, I'd get these incredible thoughts—they'd light up my mind—and I'd say to myself, "I'll write these down later when I have a pen and paper." Two hours later, when I had the appropriate tools, I had forgotten the idea. Now I write all of my ideas down, and at the end of the day or week, I comb through them to see what I've written. Even if 80% of them were trivial or repetitive, at least I've saved the gems.

One of the reasons we forget is that our memory is "state bound." If we change the state, many of the associations we have get lost. A good illustration of this is Charlie Chaplin's silent movie *City Lights*. Much of the film involves Charlie's relationship with a drunken millionaire who is constantly changing his state of mind. When they first meet one evening, Charlie saves this man's life just as he is about to commit suicide. The man befriends Charlie and takes him home. The next morning when the man has sobered up, he doesn't remember Charlie and kicks him out. The next night when the man is drunk again, he recognizes Charlie and befriends him again. This sequence happens several times, but you get the point.

One man told me that every morning when he steps into the shower, he gets what he calls "a twenty minute mental core-dump of ideas." To make sure that he doesn't lose any of these, he bought himself a piece of clear lucite plastic and a grease pencil to write them down while he's in his "think tank."

Summary

The explorer is your role for searching, looking, and probing. When you adopt this role, you venture off the beaten path, look in outside fields, and pay attention to a variety of different kinds of information. When you perform this role well, you'll pass along the makings of a new idea to the artist.

There are several reasons why some people don't go exploring. For one thing, it's easy to get stuck in the routines of daily life. To be sure, it takes energy to break out of routines, but if you don't do it, you'll get locked into where you've been and won't find anything new.

Second, the explorer runs the risk of getting lost—or worse. While discovering something that's different or unusual can be exciting and invigorating, it can also be threatening. There are some doors, that once opened, can never be closed, and you have to live with what you've found. That's a risk you must come to terms with.

A third reason for not opening up is specialization. In order to survive in the work place, many people are having to become experts on narrower and narrower subjects. Psychologist Abraham Maslow recognized the dangers of this phenomenon when he said,

People who are only good with hammers see every problem as a nail.

As a result, they are reluctant to look "outside the square" of what they know.

To perform effectively, your explorer needs to maintain his flexibility, courage, and openness.

The Explorer's Compass

Be curious.
Adopt an
"insight outlook."

**Create a map
for yourself.**
Have an idea of what
you're looking for.

Leave your own turf.
Look in outside fields,
disciplines, and industries.

Too much is not enough.
Look for lots of ideas.

Don't be afraid to be led astray.
You'll find what you weren't looking for.

Break up your routine.
Use obstacles to get out of ruts.

Shift your focus.
Pay attention to a variety of information.

Don't overlook the obvious.
What's right in front of you?

Get out your magnifying glass.
Big things come in small packages.

What does it all really mean?
Stand back and look at the Big Picture.

Slay a dragon.
Look for ideas in a place you've been avoiding.

Remember where you've been.
Trigger the ideas you already have.

Stake your claim to the new territory.
Write your idea down when you find it.

The Artist
Your role for transforming information into new ideas

Exercise: Here's an opportunity for you to use your imagination. What do these squares look like to you? Try to think of at least three different things.

Do Something To It

Some painters transform
the sun into a yellow spot,
others transform a yellow spot
into the sun.

—Pablo Picasso, Artist

One of my favorite print ads was done in the 1960's by Charles Piccirillo and Monte Ghertler (both of Doyle Dane Bernbach) to promote National Library Week. The headline consisted of the alphabet in lower case letters like so:

abcdefghijklmnopqrstuvwxyz

followed by this copy:

At your public library they've got these arranged in ways that can make you cry, giggle, love, hate, wonder, ponder and understand.

It's astonishing what those twenty-six little marks can do.

In Shakespeare's hands they become *Hamlet*. Mark Twain wound them into *Huckleberry Finn*. James Joyce twisted them into *Ulysses*. Gibbon pounded them in *The Decline and Fall of the Roman Empire*. Milton shaped them into *Paradise Lost*. Einstein added some numbers and signs (to save time and space) and they formed *The General Theory of Relativity*....

The ad continues on to extol the virtues of reading and mention that good books are available at your local library. There are several messages here, but to me the most important is that creative ideas come from manipulating and transforming your resources—no matter how few and simple they are.

To say this in another way, you'll have to *do* something to the materials your explorer has collected to give them value. As artist Jasper Johns put it when asked to describe what was involved in the creative process: "It's simple, you just take something and do something to it, and then do something else to it. Keep doing this and pretty soon you've got something."

The artist is your role for "doing something to it." You take the materials your explorer has gathered and ask, "What if I added this, or took that away, or suspended the rules, or looked at it backwards, or got a little crazy, or compared it to something else?" And pretty soon, you come up with something. In this way, you transform raw materials into new ideas and problems into opportunities.

Artists All Around Us

The artist is not a different kind of person, but every person is a different kind of artist.

—Eric Gill, Philosopher

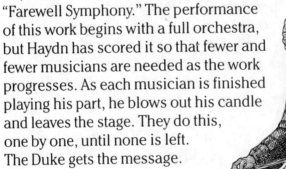

Often when we think of artists, we think of painters, musicians, and dancers. But the artist's mindset of "doing something to it" can be employed by anyone to their own benefit. Here are some examples of artists at work.

The musicians of Franz Josef Haydn's orchestra are mad at the Duke because he's promised them a vacation but has postponed it a number of times. They ask Haydn to complain to the Duke about getting them some time off. Haydn thinks for a bit, decides that music should do the talking, and composes the "Farewell Symphony." The performance of this work begins with a full orchestra, but Haydn has scored it so that fewer and fewer musicians are needed as the work progresses. As each musician is finished playing his part, he blows out his candle and leaves the stage. They do this, one by one, until none is left. The Duke gets the message.

Dale Strumpell is the sound designer for the science fiction motion picture *2010*. His job is to come up with the sound of a spaceship's high speed deceleration in the atmosphere of Jupiter. Where do you get a sound like this? Well, you play around a bit. After several experiments, he takes some dry ice and puts it on a piece of sheet metal. He ignites a blow torch underneath, and puts a microphone nearby. The quick melting of the dry ice gives him exactly the sound he's searching for.

What's a nanosecond? It's a billionth of a second (10^{-9}), and it's the basic time interval of a supercomputer's internal clock. Navy Commander Grace Hopper has to explain the meaning of a nanosecond to some non-technical computer users. She wonders, "How can I get them to understand the brevity of a nanosecond? Why not look at it as a space problem rather than a time problem? I'll just use the distance light can travel in one billionth of a second." She pulls out a piece of string 11.8 inches (30 cm.) long and tells her visitors, "Here is one nanosecond."

It's the second century B.C., and a young Greek librarian is trying to think of a more efficient way to order and retrieve the thousands of manuscripts that he has stored away. "How should I order these?" he wonders. "By subject? By author? By color?" Then he thinks of the alphabet. His contemporaries think of it simply as a series of phonetic symbols— *alpha, beta, gamma, delta, epsilon*—that create words when joined together. This librarian decides to de-emphasize the alphabet's linguistic qualities and emphasize solely the letters' order in relation to one another. He puts all the documents beginning with *gamma* after those beginning with *beta* but in front of those beginning with *delta*. In the process, he creates alpha-betization, the primary means for ordering, storing, and retrieving information.

Stanley Marsh wants to landscape the driveway of his Texas ranch. He also wants something more exciting than your typical plants, rocks, and shrubs. He thinks about various alternatives and then sees a late '50's Cadillac drive by—the kind with the huge tail fins. Inspiration strikes! He likes what he sees and buys up a bunch of the cars. He then buries them headfirst at an angle along his driveway every twenty feet or so, and his landscaping is complete. In the process, he creates a "national landmark."

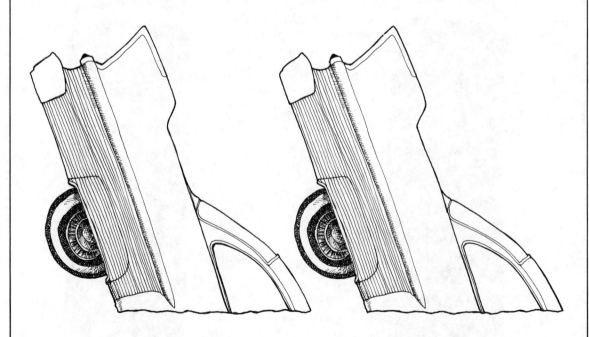

This then is what being an artist is all about: *changing patterns, looking at things in different ways, and experimenting with various approaches.* In this way, melting dry ice becomes a decelerating space ship, the alphabet is converted into an ordering device, strike grievances are transformed into symphonies, tailfins are changed into landscaping, and nanoseconds become string.

Speaking of "doing something to it," how did you do with the squares exercise at the beginning of this chapter? At face value the picture appears to be a series of various shaded squares. But if you play with the problem you might come up with ideas like:

☞ A quilt

☞ Nestling cubes

☞ Aerial photograph of Nebraska farmland

☞ Six shades of gray

☞ Maze constructed by a psychotic

☞ Population density chart

☞ Heat distribution pattern

All of these are good descriptions. Notice, though, that most of them focus on the squares. If you turn it upside down and step back about twenty feet, you'll find that you're no longer describing the squares, but something else—in this case the face of Abraham Lincoln.

In the same way a painter has a variety of colors on his palette, a good artist will have a variety of strategies for transforming his materials. I have included in this chapter some of my favorite techniques for manipulating ideas.

They are:

Adapt	Compare
Imagine	Eliminate
Reverse	Parody
Connect	Incubate

I encourage you to try them all and discover which ones work best for you.

Adapt: Change Contexts

Exercise: Let's suppose that you're the marketing manager for a manufacturing company. 🌑 You get a call from the president and learn that somehow the 🌑 corporate inventory system has fouled up, and the company now has $1,000,000 worth of ball bearings it doesn't need. Furthermore, you can't return them to the vendor. Your task is to think of things to do with the ball bearings, using them either one-at-a-time or in combinations. What are your ideas? 🌑 Take a minute and list them.

Here are some possibilities:

🌑 Use them as level testers.

🌑 Make furniture out of them—like bean bag chairs—to be used in public places. Since they'd be heavy, they wouldn't get stolen.

🌑 Serve them as robot caviar (when your "home robot" is having friends over).

🌑 Sew them into a canvas vest and use them as "weight clothing" for runners-in-training.

🌑 Put them on the bottom of uneven curtains and use them as curtain weights.

🌑 Use them as confetti at a punk rock concert.

🌑 Make jewelry out of them: earrings, bracelets, and necklaces.

🌑 Use them as a promotional gimmick: put them in a jar and see who can guess how many there are.

The point is that an idea, object, or thing 🌑 in this case a ball bearing—takes its meaning from the context in which you put it. If you change its context, it will take on a different meaning. For example, transferring a ball bearing from the "things that reduce friction" 🌑 context to that of "shiny and pretty things" gives us all kinds 🌑 of jewelry and art ideas. Emphasizing its "mass" characteristics allows us to think of "weight" ideas, such as curtain weights 🌑 and ballast for a ship.

Changing contexts 🌑 is an important way to discover the possibilities of your resources. For example, I'm holding a pen. Viewed one way, it's a writing device. If I think about it in other ways, it's a weapon, a pointer, an ear cleaner, or a door stop.

As long as I emphasize different parts of it and allow myself to change contexts, I'll think of new ideas. Similarly, I remember on my daughter's third birthday, I gave her a small box with a dozen colored cubes in it. She picked it up, shook it, and told me that it was a rattle. She opened it up and said that it was a wallet and the cubes were money. Then she piled the cubes up, and they became a birthday cake. In a like vein, consider the first person who looked at waste sawdust and thought "compressed fire log," or looked at petrochemical goop and thought "silly putty," or who saw an artichoke and thought "food."

Exercise: Shown below is the Roman numeral seven. By adding only a single line, turn it into an eight.

VII

This is pretty easy; all you have to do is add a vertical line to the right of the VII to create an eight—like so—VIII. Want something a little more challenging? Shown below is a Roman numeral nine. By adding only a single line, turn it into a 6.

IX

Some people put an horizontal line through the center, turn it upside down, and then cover the bottom. This gives you a Roman numeral VI. A more artistic solution might be to put "S" in front of the IX to create "SIX." What we've done here is take the IX out of the context of Roman numerals and put it into the context of "Arabic numerals spelled out in English." The thing that prevents some people from doing this is that even with only three examples of Roman numerals—VII, VIII, and IX—they get locked into the context of Roman numerals.

 One of the explorer's tips is to look for the second right answer. Can you think of any other ways you can add a single line to "IX" and turn it into a 6?

IX

Another solution might be to add the line "6" after the IX. Then you get IX6, or one times six. Here the "X" no longer represents "10" or the English letter "X" but rather the multiplication sign. Everybody has a lot of knowledge; by shifting the contexts in which you think about it, you'll discover new ideas.

Imagine: Ask What If

Exercise: What if dog food manufacturers put non-digestable additives—for example, petunia or marigold seeds—in their products? Dogs would then become delivery systems going about planting and fertilizing flowers. Another additive might be a non-toxic fluorescent material. This would be especially appropriate in cities at night where pedestrians would know that the object glowing in the dark up ahead is something they don't want to step in. What other additives can you think of?

I have a friend whom I talk to about the creative process. She thinks that my ideas are interesting but that "what really happens in the inner chamber of creative thought is indistinguishable from magic." She makes a good point. If you stop to think about it, our thinking is magical. We can think about everything from quarks and the square root of -1 to fantasy planets and dream vacations. It's this magical ability to think about imaginary ideas that gives the artist much of his power.

An easy way to use this type of thinking is to simply ask,

What if _____ ?

and then fill in the blank with some contrary-to-fact or non-existing situation. Don't worry about being practical. As a matter of fact, be as imaginative as you can. Often we have so many assumptions built up about the way things should be that we can only skirt them with an unusual "what if" question. The next step is to answer the question. While you do this, remember to keep your judge at a distance and withhold critical evaluation. That's because although many of the ideas you come up with won't be very practical, these impractical ideas can act as *stepping stones* to usable, creative ideas. Sometimes crazy, foolish, or weird ideas can lead to practical ideas and the only way you would have found them is by going over the *stepping stone.*

For example, suppose you're an architect trying to think up design ideas for a new office building, and you ask yourself, "What if the outsides of buildings were covered with fur like animals? Would they be easier to heat and cool? Perhaps they would shed in the summer. Maybe they could be groomed to reflect the state of mind of their dwellers. Military bases might have crew cuts. Retirement villages might be tinted gray. College dorms might have long hair." You play with this for awhile, and then your mind skips to another animal, namely snakes. You start thinking how their scales fit together. This ultimately gives you some ideas for a roof tiling pattern that's both energy efficient and pleasing to look at.

Here are some what-if's for you to think about:

☞ What if income tax roulette were established, that is, the percentage rate at which your income is taxed would be determined by a chance spin of a roulette wheel? What would happen? Would the Treasury Department treat people with big incomes like "high rollers?" Would there be citizens' initiatives asking for additional "double zeroes" on the roulette wheel?

☞ What if customer service were our #1 priority instead of profits? Would year-end bonuses be based on decreased complaints? We'd really have to get inside our customer's heads and anticipate what kinds of products they'd like to have next year.

☞ What if everyone had a set limit on the number of words they could utter in their lifetime? Would we be more precise? What would happen to politicians? Would we find other ways to express ourselves? Would clothing be brighter and more expressive? Would telepathy have developed?

☞ What if people were able to do all their mundane chores such as mowing the lawn, washing the dishes, or painting the fence in their sleep?

☞ What if people stopped showing outward signs of aging when they reached forty?

☞ What if for five minutes every month people could turn into their favorite plant or vegetable?

☞ What if people had edible clothes? Perhaps fashions would change as different foods came into season. Taking someone out to lunch could have new meanings. You might say such things as, "Would you like to eat my socks? Did you buy your wardrobe at Safeway?" Putting your foot in your mouth would taste better.

☞ What if cats sold life insurance to birds?

☞ What if every high school biology student had their own cadaver to work on? They'd get to know a person inside out. They'd also learn the importance of taking good care of their bodies first hand.

Tip: Make up your own what-if questions and see where they lead your imagination. The more you do it, the better you'll get, and the more likely you'll find something worthwhile.

Reverse: Look At It Backwards

Life is tough. It takes up all your time, all your week-ends, and what do you get at the end of it? Death, a great reward. I think the life cycle is all backwards. You should die first, get it out of the way, then you live for twenty years in an old age home. You get kicked out when you're too young, receive a gold watch, and you go to work. You work for forty years until you're young enough to enjoy your retirement. You go to college, you do drugs, alcohol, you party until you're ready for high school. You go to high school, grade school, you become a little kid, you play, you have no responsibilities, you become a little baby, you go back into the womb, you spend your last nine months float-ing, and you finish off as a gleam in someone's eye.
—Anonymous comedian.

Exercise: An eccentric old king wants to bequeath his throne to one of his two sons. He decides that a horse race will be run and that the son who owns the slower horse will become king. The sons, each fearing that the other will cheat by having his horse go less fast than it is capable of, ask a wise man's advice. With only two words the wise man tells them how to make sure that the race will be fair. What are the two words?

Reversing your perspective on a problem is a good technique for opening up your thinking. Here's an example of how such a strategy can work. Carl Djerassi, one of the developers of the birth control pill in the 1950's, is the head of a pesticide company. As such, he's concerned about the adverse health and economic effects certain insects have on society. Like many other scientists, he's also concerned about the harmful side-effects that many pesticides have had on the environment. He asks himself, "How can I eliminate harmful insects without harming the environment?" He plays with his objective and decides to focus not on *death* but on *birth*. "What if rather than killing the insects we prevent them from being born in the first place? If we could give them specially-targeted hormones that would prevent their sex organs from reaching maturity, they wouldn't be able to reproduce themselves." This is the approach he takes, and it works.

Suppose you're a teacher and you wonder, "How can I be less effective?" This would mean that the student would have to take more responsibility for his learning, and this could lead to the development of a self-study go-at-your-own-pace program.

Suppose you're designing a solar cell. Posing the problem as an attempt to raise efficiency to 30% would lead your thinking in one direction, while asking how to reduce inefficiency to 70% would lead your thinking to a very different destination. Similarly, the shift in focus from "cure" to "prevention" in stating medical goals has changed the field of medicine.

Tip: Look in the opposite direction. You'll see the things you usually don't look at. It's also a good way to free your thinking from deeply embedded assumptions.* Try this on for size. Write three paragraphs describing a concept you're currently developing. Here's the twist: if you're a male, write it from the point of view of a female; if you're a female write it from a male's point of view. At the very least, you'll create some interesting stepping stones.

---

*Of course, perceiving things backwards is not without its problems. The story goes that William Spooner (the late nineteenth century English educator known for transposing the initial sounds of words, e.g., *tons of soil* for *sons of toil* or *queer old dean* for *dear old queen,* and from whom we get the term *Spoonerism*) was at a dinner party in which he happened to knock the salt shaker on the carpet. Without missing a beat, Spooner poured his wine on top of it.

Connect: Join Together

The philosopher Rene Descartes went into a bar and sat down. The bartender asked him if he'd like a beer. Decartes replied, "I think not," and disappeared.

You probably wouldn't think the above joke was very funny unless you were able to *connect* it to the fact that the foundation of Descartes' philosophy was his statement, "I think, therefore I am." However, not only humor relies on making connections. It's also the basis of invention, poetry, air travel, business success, and crime detection. As design critic Ralph Caplan has put it, "All art, and most knowledge, entails either seeing connections or making them. Until it is hooked up with what you already know, nothing can ever be learned or assimilated."

Much of creative thinking also involves connecting two previously unconnected ideas and turning them into something new. Gutenberg connected the idea of the coin punch and the wine press to create moveable type and the printing press. Gregor Mendel connected mathematics with biology to create the field of genetics. Fred Smith connected the airlines' "hub and spoke" distribution idea with that of an overnight package delivery service to create Federal Express.

A fun use of the trigger concepts listed in the explorer chapter is to choose several of them and connect them together to see what kinds of ideas their combined associations spark. For example:

Maze + Water =

☆ A river working its way from the mountains to the sea

☆ Veins of living things

☆ 19th century attempts to find the source of the Nile River

☆ A submarine running an obstacle course

Magnet + Library =

☆ A "pull" or incentive to get people to return overdue books, perhaps allowing them access to a rare book room

☆ A bookstore having a sale

☆ A beautiful woman or handsome man (their genetic "library" has given them an attractive appearance)

Tool + Mattress =

☆ A device for football players to practice blocking

☆ A drug to stimulate dreams

☆ A place to practice jumping

Sandpaper + Ring =

☆ A tool for polishing round objects

☆ A war maneuver such as a siege in which a city is encircled and then slowly ground down

☆ Richard Wagner's *Ring* cycle: four long operas that wear the audience down

What would you do with Rainbow + Clock? Script + Brakes? Satellite + Parasite? Sometimes nothing will happen. Sometimes you'll get a good idea. Have fun trying.

Ask yourself: What ideas can I connect to my concept?

Compare: Make A Metaphor

Shall I compare thee to a summer's day?

—William Shakespeare, Playwright

Exercise: Try the following.

1. Eating a fine dinner is like:

   A) Throwing the javelin a long distance.

   B) Watching an hourglass drip sand.

   C) Reading a popular novel at the beach.

   D) Putting fingernail polish on your toes.

2. Raising a child is like:

   A) Driving from Seattle to New York.

   B) Weeding your garden.

   C) Building a fire and watching it burn.

   D) Fishing for rainbow trout.

3. Playing a piano recital is like:

   A) Investing in the stock market.

   B) Growing orchids.

   C) Driving through rush hour traffic
       with your gas gauge on E.

   D) Fasting for three days.

4. Finding truth is like:

   A) Making banana nut bread.

   B) Walking into a room and forgetting the reason why.

   C) Navigating a sailboat through a violent thunderstorm.

   D) Taking a test that has no wrong answers.

How did you do? Well, no matter what you put down, you got the right answer. That's because the purpose of this exercise was for you to find some similarity between the different ideas. Whether you think raising a child is like weeding a garden or playing a piano recital is like investing, you were able to find something that the ideas had in common.

This is what making metaphors is all about: finding similarity. You take one idea and use it to describe another idea because of some similarity the two share. We use this type of thinking all the time. We say that roads have "shoulders," hammers have "heads," computers have "footprints," minds have "frames," ideas are "half-baked," batteries go "dead," cities have "hearts," and candidates have "landslide" victories. As a matter of fact, many discoveries have been made because someone found a new metaphor to describe a situation.

In the 17th century, William Harvey looked at the heart not as a muscle or an organ, but as a "pump," and discovered the circulation of blood. In the early 20th century, the Danish physicist Niels Bohr developed a new model of the atom by comparing it to the solar system. Within this framework, he figured that the sun represented the nucleus and the planets represented the electrons. With this model, he supplanted the Rutherford "raisin pudding" model of the atom.

Sometimes, a metaphor can give you a fresh insight into a problem. For example, several years ago I had a computer client that couldn't understand why its sales were flat in the middle of a boom market. Because they were too close to the situation to have any perspective, we made a metaphor for the problem. We decided that their company was like a full service restaurant. Its menu (product line) was large but there were too many restrictions on what could be bought—for example, a customer couldn't order salad with pork. Since the individual cooks (division managers) decided what items were on the menu, there was no consistency in their offerings. This led to specialized waiters (salesmen). A typical result? A patron couldn't buy fish from a steak waiter. We developed this metaphor further, but it quickly became clear to management that their large, restricted product line confused their customers and was the source of their flat sales.

The Bible is quite metaphorical. Whether it's Jesus talking in parables, St. Paul sprinkling his epistles with similes, or the Prophets foretelling the future, you will find many ideas expressed in metaphors. This is especially true in the Book of *Proverbs.* Here's a quick quiz for you from *Proverbs*. Connect the metaphor on the left side with the idea it represents on the right side.

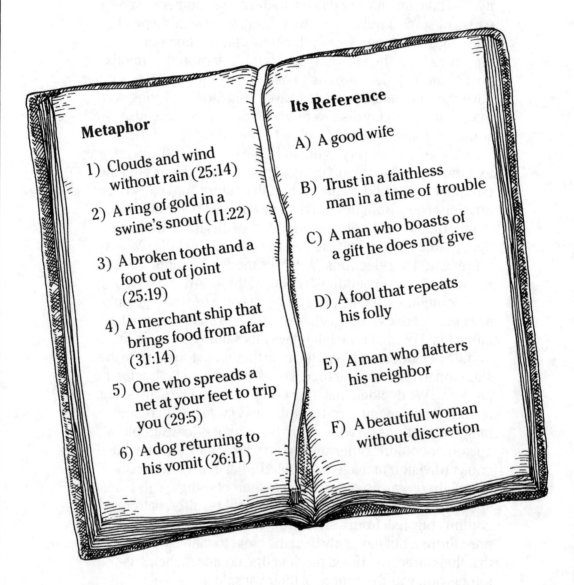

Metaphor

1) Clouds and wind without rain (25:14)

2) A ring of gold in a swine's snout (11:22)

3) A broken tooth and a foot out of joint (25:19)

4) A merchant ship that brings food from afar (31:14)

5) One who spreads a net at your feet to trip you (29:5)

6) A dog returning to his vomit (26:11)

Its Reference

A) A good wife

B) Trust in a faithless man in a time of trouble

C) A man who boasts of a gift he does not give

D) A fool that repeats his folly

E) A man who flatters his neighbor

F) A beautiful woman without discretion

Exercise: You'll need a pencil, paper, and a watch for this. Shown below are two lists. Take a minute (time yourself) and memorize the words in list one. Then take a minute and write down as many as you can remember. Repeat the process for list two.

List One:	List Two:
same	sunset
loss	mirror
certain	brick
deficit	diamond
term	wishbone
comma	cow
about	roses
send	umbrella
quantity	monkey
determine	pretzel
phase	goblet
labor	castle
sequence	guitar
set	wristwatch
very	pencil
appendix	oil can

How did you do? I've found that most people remember more words from the second list. One reason is that the words in list two are more visual. You can make a picture in your mind of a guitar-playing monkey standing in front of a castle. Then when you need to remember the items, you just look at the picture.

I bring this up in connection with metaphors because most metaphors are visual. Thus, if you can make a metaphor for what you want to remember, you're less likely to forget it. For example, some years ago, I had to memorize the various parts of a computer operating system. I didn't want to memorize all the details but I did need to know the various relationships of the parts to one another. So I said to myself, "This operating system is like an automobile. This part is like the chassis, this part is like the engine, this part is like the steering wheel, and so on." Whenever I needed to remember the operating system, I just brought to mind a picture of an automobile.

Tip: I've found that some of the easiest metaphors to develop are those in which there is some action taking place. Here's a list of potential candidates. Try comparing your situation to one or more of these:

Cooking a meal	Driving a car
Giving a speech	Planting a garden
Pruning a tree	Writing a story
Making a deal	Shooting at a target
Spreading propaganda	Starting a revolution
Promoting a product	Conducting an orchestra
Raising a child	Fighting a fire
Waging a war	Prospecting for gold
Going fishing	Solving a problem
Managing a project	Looking at the stars
Colonizing a territory	Reading a novel
Planning a vacation	Following a religion
Competing in track	Having a baby
Making a sales call	Performing a magic trick
Building a house	Arranging flowers

How is cooking a meal like giving a speech? How is solving a problem like having a baby? How is managing a project like planning a vacation? Have fun mixing these ideas.*

---

*Sometimes people mix their metaphors in unusual ways. This can lead not only to logical inconsistencies, but also to humorous, almost surreal images. Oregon professor Roland Bartel likes to collect mixed metaphors. Here are some of his favorites: "I prefer the long distance runner to the short term band aid." "We're all going down the drain in a steamroller." "It's just a matter of whose ox is being goosed." "A virgin forest is one in which the hand of man has not set foot." "We've got to be careful about getting too many cooks in this soup or somebody's going to think there's dirty work behind the cross roads."

Eliminate: Break The Rules

If you don't ask "why this?" often
enough, somebody will ask "why you?"

—Tom Hirshfield, Inventor

Slaying sacred cows makes great steaks.

—Dick Nicolosi, Philosopher

Exercise: Shown below is a maze. Starting at point A, work
your way through to point B. Use a pen or pencil to keep track
of your progress.

That wasn't too difficult. Now take a look at what you've done. To solve this problem, you probably used one of the following three strategies. The first is, you started at A and worked your way through to B. Whenever you came to a dead end, you backtracked out of it and then moved forward anew. A second approach is to start at B and move backwards to A. We use this method for much of what we do. If you have a project that must be finished three months from today, you might think to yourself, "Where should I be in two months? Where should I be next month? Where should I be next week?"

A third solution is to break the rules. How about drawing a straight line from point A to point B? Maybe going all the way around the border? How about tearing the page out of the book and folding it in half so that B touches A? Some people object that breaking the rules goes against the directions. That may be true but sometimes you have to do that in order to be innovative. As educator Rudolph Flesch put it:

Creative thinking may simply mean the realization that there's no particular virtue in doing things the way they have always been done.

Look at sports. If people hadn't changed the rules along the way, there would still be a jump ball after every field goal in basketball, foul balls wouldn't count as strikes in baseball, and football would still have only a running game. Indeed, most advances in science, technology, design, homemaking, medicine, and agriculture have come about when someone has either broken the rules or temporarily suspended them. With his air conditioner, Willis Carrier broke the rule that offices had to be hot in summer. With her passionate love odes, Sappho broke the rule that only men could write good lyric poetry. With his formulation that the sum of the angles of a triangle doesn't have to add up to 180°, Karl Gauss broke the rule that the only type of geometry was Euclidean geometry. With his lightning attacks of mechanized equipment, Rommel broke the rules on how to fight a battle. With his multi-million dollar advertising rollout for Lotus 1-2-3, Mitch Kapor broke the rules on how to introduce microcomputer software into the marketplace.

A banker I know likes this link between elimination and innovation. He asked the eight people reporting to him to write down five things they didn't like about their jobs—policies, procedures, ways of dealing with customers, etc. Curiously, all eight people had three similar things on their lists. They focused on these, and were able to eliminate two of them as being obsolete. You might try this yourself. What are five things you don't like about your current operations? Can any of these be eliminated as obsolete?

An accountant told me about a similar strategy he employs to cut down on paperwork. Every month he prepares a number of financial reports that he then sends out to the people on his routing list. He always completes the reports on time, but every six months or so, he'll send them out several days late to see who "squawks" about not getting the information on time. If people complain, then he knows that the report is important for them to do their jobs. If they don't complain, he questions whether they still need that particular report to be generated. He's been able to eliminate a lot of out-of-date paperwork as a result of this practice.

Exercise: You're the director of a TV commercial for an automobile that will be broadcast to a nationwide audience. What are five "rules" you can break in how you portray the product?

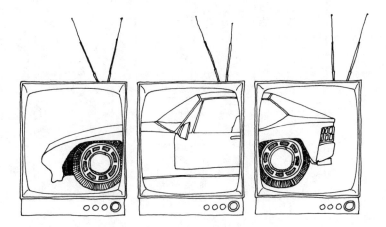

Tip: Break the rules. If you usually start shaving on the left side of your face, tomorrow start on the right. If you never watch soap operas, watch some daytime television. If you usually listen to jazz, then listen to classical music. If you usually take the fast way home from work, take the slower scenic route.

Parody: Fool Around

Imagination was given to man to compensate him for what he is not. A sense of humor was provided to console him for what he is.

—Horace Walpole, Man of Letters

Exercise: What if people slept in their refrigerators? You'd probably dream about skiing and snowball fights. And you'd put your head in the freezer for a deep sleep. People who usually stuffed their money in their mattresses would have cold cash. And those with frigidity problems would have a good excuse. "Not tonight dear, I have a head cold." Many refrigerators are self-cleaning. Maybe it wouldn't be necessary to bathe. What else would happen?

When we think of an artist, we sometimes think of a sculptor working with clay. Occasionally, the artist needs a little silly putty, and that's where his next tool, fooling around, comes in. The artist uses humor and absurd what-if questions to loosen himself up and look at things in a fresh way. For example, he might tell a joke or two:

Question: What do you call a clairvoyant midget who just broke out of prison?

Answer: A small medium at large.

Question: What's the last thing to go through a bug's mind the instant he smashes into your windshield?

Answer: His rear end.

Question: Why did the explorer pay twenty dollars for a sheet of sand paper?

Answer: He thought it was a map of the Sahara Desert.

Or, he might give you a new set of conversion factors:

10^{12} microphones = 1 megaphone

10^{12} pins = 1 terrapin

$3\frac{1}{3}$ tridents = 1 decadent

4 seminaries = 1 binary

10^{21} picolos = 1 gigolo

1 milli-Helen = the amount of beauty required to launch 1 ship

He might quote Margaret Thornley or Strange de Jim (as Herb Caen has done):

Beet ever so onion there snow peas legume.

—Margaret Thornley, Pun Artist

I don't like to eat snails. I prefer fast food.

—Strange de Jim, Pundit

Or he might give you a menu with the following list of ducks:

Cold Duck
Peking Duck
Duck Soup
Sitting Duck
Wild Duck
Conducktor
Pas de Dux

The artist believes that there is a close relation between the *ha-ha* experience of humor and the *aha!* experience of creative discovery. If you can laugh at something, then you're more likely to challenge the rules underlying the idea and look at it in unusual ways. This is borne out by a creativity test that was given to a group of high school students a few years ago. The participants were divided into two equal groups. One group sat silently in a study hall for half an hour prior to the test. The other group spent the same time in another room listening to a tape recording of a standup comedian. Then both groups took the creativity test. The group that had listened to the comedy did significantly better in all phases of the test. The comedy had opened up their thinking.

One of my clients, a satellite manufacturer, had a design meeting in which everyone got into a crazy frame of mind and decided to roast the satellite. They made up jokes and had a lot of fun. The result: they came up with a lot of good design ideas. The next week, when everyone in the group was quite serious, they came up with no new ideas.

Exercise: You're the mayor of your city. What are three things about your city which you can make fun of?

Tip: Fool around. Listen to comedy albums. Read joke books to get in a creative frame of mind. Humor is especially effective when your artist is stuck or under a lot of pressure. As physicist Niels Bohr put it, "There are some things that are so serious that you have to laugh at them."

Incubate: Do Nothing

Learn to pause … or nothing worthwhile will catch up to you.

—Doug King, Poet

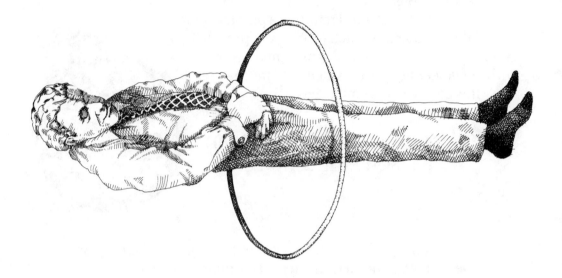

Exercise: Take a minute and think of seven people who went to high school with you.

It's tough to see the good ideas behind you by focusing twice as hard at things in front of you. Sometimes letting go and turning the problem over to the active powers of your unconscious can be the best strategy of all. As software developer Rick Tendy says, "I never try to solve a problem by trying to solve it."

By putting the idea on your mental back burner, you allow three beneficial things to take place. First, you put your problem in perspective. One advertising man told me that his strategy for coming up with ideas is to spend five or six weeks inundating himself with information about the client and its market. Then he'll go fishing for three days, and "let the ideas percolate their way to the top." To draw an analogy to the Lincoln exercise you did at the beginning of this chapter, we spend most of our time "thinking in the squares." But if you can back away from the situation, you'll see the big picture.

Second, when you work on a problem, you plant a seed in your mind. When you back away, this seed continues to grow. It sends its roots out in your gray matter and makes new connections. For example, how did you do with the high school classmate exercise? It wasn't too difficult. But now that the problem has been planted in your mind, you'll think of seven more when you wake up tomorrow morning, and continue to think—at least unconsciously—of more after that.

Third, when you return to a problem or idea after incubating, you'll probably approach it with somewhat different assumptions. An engineering vice president told me that his advice to his employees is:

One o'clock should mean something new.

Some of his people spend all of their time focusing directly on the problem. They'll work on it all morning, and when noon comes, they'll bring out their brown bag lunches and continue to work on it. At one o'clock, they continue to work on it, and as a result, they bring no fresh perspective to the problem. The vice president encourages his people to go to lunch, to exercise, or to go to the library—anything to break set.

One last note on incubation: sometimes delaying action will give you more information. Designer Christopher Williams tells the following story about an architect who built a cluster of large office buildings that were set in a central green. When construction was completed, the landscape crew asked him where he wanted the sidewalks between the buildings. "Not yet," was the architect's reply, "just plant the grass solidly between the buildings." This was done, and by late summer the new lawn was laced with pathways of trodden grass, connecting building to building, and building to outside. As Williams puts it, "The paths followed the most efficient line between the points of connection, turned in easy curves rather than right angles, and were sized according to traffic flow. In the fall the architect simply paved in the pathways. Not only did the pathways have a design beauty, but they responded directly to user needs."

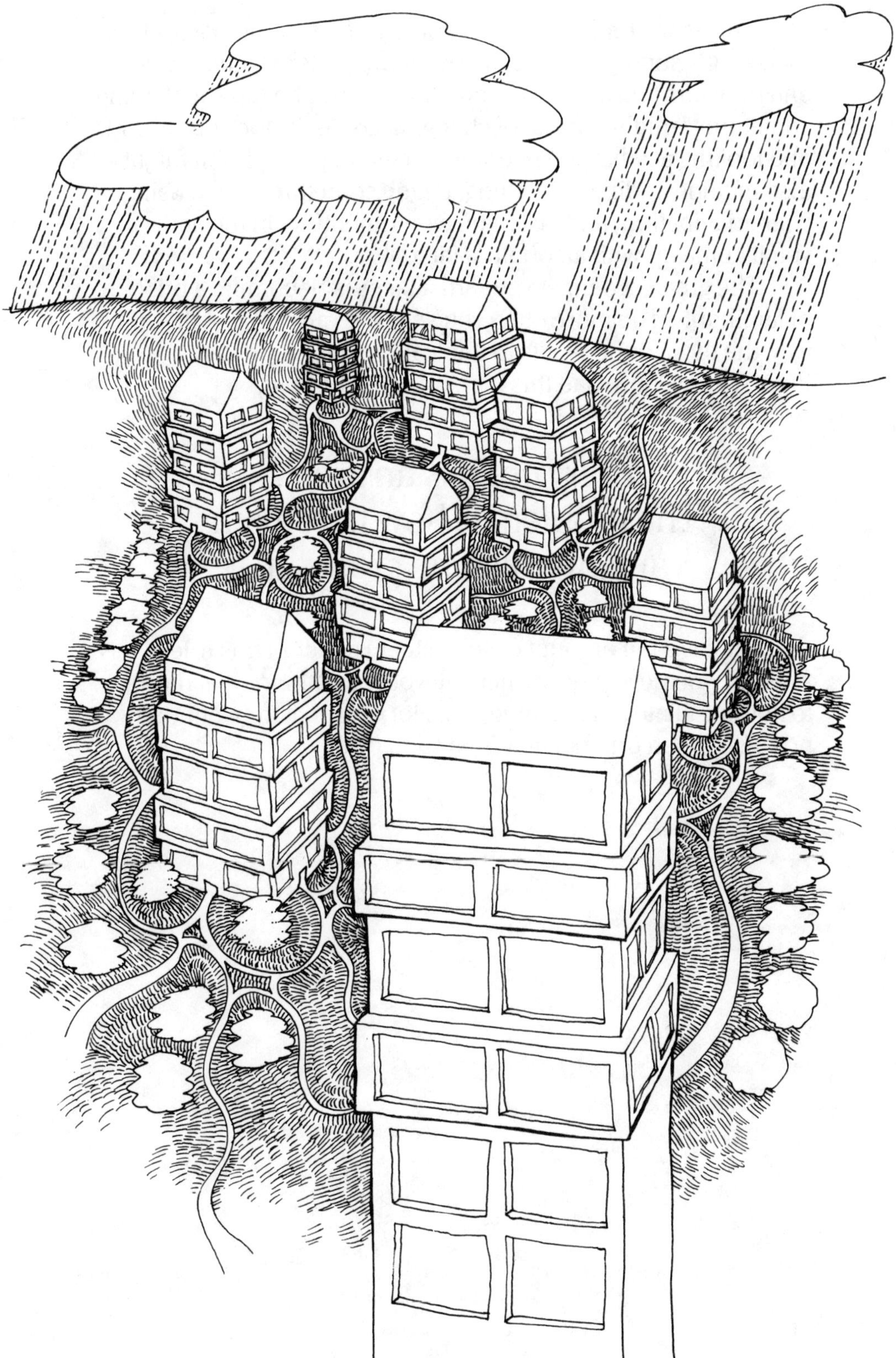

Summary

The artist is your role for "doing something" to your materials, for taking a sundry group of information, patterns, and ideas and transforming them into something new. The tools for "doing something" might consist of changing contexts, fooling around, and looking at what you're doing from strange angles. It might also include adding something, taking something away, using your imagination, and just plain experimenting. In the end, you'll come up with an original idea.

The greatest danger your artist faces is becoming a prisoner of familiarity. The more often you see or do anything in the same way, the more difficult it is to think about it in any other way. Picasso must have had this in mind when he said,

Every child is an artist.
The problem is how to remain
an artist after he grows up.

It takes a fair amount of self-esteem to adopt this role. After all, you never know where all your "doing" may lead you: to nothing at all (wasted time), to a lot of criticism (wounded pride), or to an original new idea (bingo!).

The Artist's Palette

Take your concept and "do" something to it. What patterns can you change? How can you alter the way you think about it?

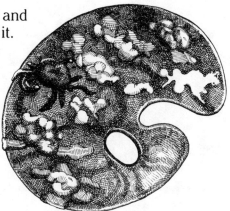

Adapt. What different contexts can you put your concept in? What historical contexts? What futuristic ones? What unusual geographical or political contexts could you make it a part of?

Imagine. What unusual what-if questions can you make up involving your concept? How far-out can you go? How surreal?

Reverse. Look at your concept backwards. How does it look upside down? Or inside out?

Connect. What can you combine with your concept? How does your concept fit in with the rest of your knowledge?

Compare. Make a metaphor for your concept. What similarities does it share with music? Medicine? Warfare? Cooking? Gardening? Traveling? Courting?

Eliminate. What rules can you break? What's obsolete? What's taboo? What's no longer necessary?

Parody. Make fun of your concept. Let your stupid monitor down and roast it. How silly can you be? How outrageous? What jokes can you think up involving your concept?

Incubate. What ideas are you working on that it would pay you to pause for a little bit?

The Judge

Your role for evaluating an idea
and deciding what to do with it

Exercise: Shown below is the design for a new coffee cup.
Write down three impressions you have about its value.

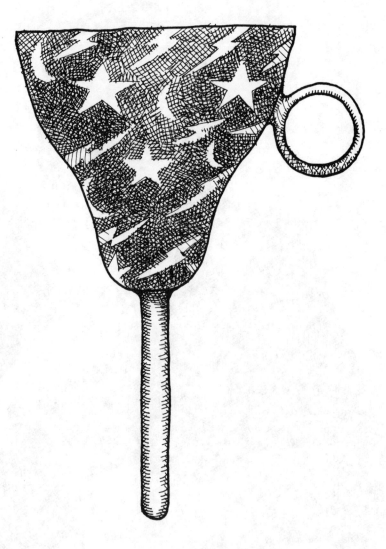

Design for a new coffee cup.

Is The Idea An Aha! Or An Uh-oh?

Play is what I do for a living;
the work comes in
evaluating the results of the play.
—Mac MacDougall, Computer Architect

You've got an idea that you'd like to turn into a reality. It could be a sketch for a painting, a business plan for a startup company, a new way to prepare chicken, an idea for a fundraising event for a local charity, or a different database structure. Now you're wondering: "How good is this idea? Will it work? Is it worth my time to pursue it further? What are the risks? Will it give me the result I want? What's the downside? Will I end up a bum or a hero?"

One way you can find out is to execute your idea and see what happens. This approach works well enough when the idea is small and the consequences of failure aren't significant. But you don't have that luxury for most ideas. So, now you need to think like a judge.

We're all familiar with the judge; indeed, it's probably our most well-developed role. We use it to evaluate everything from what clothes to wear and what books to read to deciding where to spend our vacation and how we should invest our money.

The judge's role in the creative process is a delicate one. You have to be critical enough to insure that you give your warrior an idea that's worth fighting for. But you also need to be open enough so you don't stifle your artist's imagination. If you're not critical enough, the warrior may end up getting hurt; if you're not open enough, the artist may not be creative. In addition, you have to figure out how long you have to make your decision. Indeed, much of the judge's art consists in knowing which decisions should take six seconds and which ones should take six months.

This chapter takes a look at some of the beliefs, attitudes, and assumptions that can affect your judge's ability to make good decisions.

What's Wrong With This Idea?

The human mind likes a strange idea as little as the body likes a strange protein and resists it with a similar energy.

—W.I. Beveridge, Scientist

When your judge evaluates a new idea, he'll ask such questions as: "Will it succeed? How much does it cost? How long will it take to implement? Is there a market for this? Are there resources available? Will it be fun? What will I learn from it? Will it lead to other opportunities?" In the course of this probing, your judge should scrutinize the new idea very carefully and find out what's wrong with it. But here's a word of caution: some judges go too far and focus exclusively on the new idea's faults and drawbacks.

What were your comments about the new coffee cup design? If you're like a lot of people, you probably said something like:

☞ The center of gravity is too high.

☞ You can't set it down.

☞ It looks like it would break.

☞ The handle is too small.

☞ It isn't designed right.

☞ Crummy aesthetics.

Notice that all of these comments are negative. Many people don't even ask where the cup will be used. What if it were to be used on the moon or underwater? On the beach or in a table with holes in it, as on an airplane or ship?

Your judge should know that in addition to finding out what's wrong with an idea, he should also tell you what's worth building on and offer some imaginative ways to do so. A good judge knows that sometimes a drawback in an idea—if interesting enough—can serve as a stepping stone to a practical, creative idea. With a constructive attitude, he might look at the coffee cup and say:

✔ That's good, the grounds would settle where you'd never taste them.

✔ It would be great on the beach—just stick it in the sand.

✔ It would be the perfect thing to stick through the railing of a ship.

✔ It might allow precise pre-measuring of condiments like cream, honey, sugar, or whiskey.

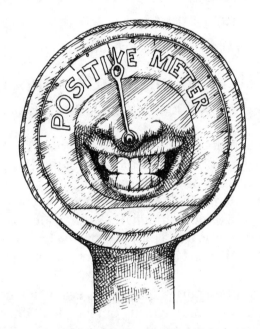

Your judge should remember that his overall purpose is to help get good ideas produced, not to revel in the beauty of his criticism. To counteract a natural negative bias, you should focus initially on the positive and interesting features of a new idea. The negative will come easily enough.

Tip: The playwright Jerome Lawrence has an evaluation technique—he calls it the "creative no"—that he uses whenever he's collaborating with someone else. It works like this: either member of the partnership can veto the other's ideas. However, when one partner does exercise this veto, he also takes responsibility for coming up with a new idea that both partners like. Thus, it's not only destructive, it's constructive as well.

What If It Fails?

◇ A ship in port is safe, but that's not what ships are built for.
—Grace Hopper, Inventor

◇ There's as much risk in doing nothing as in doing something.
—Trammell Crow, Real Estate Developer

◇ No one ever achieved greatness by playing it safe.
—Harry Gray, Business Executive

◇ I wish I'd drunk more champagne.
—Last words of John Maynard Keynes, Economist

Every venture has its risks. Whether you're choosing colors for your living room walls or bidding for the TV rights to the next Olympics, there is always the possibility of failure. Maybe the store clerk will mix the paint incorrectly. Maybe you're bidding way too much, or not enough. Risk is as much a part of the creative process as it is a part of crossing the street or falling in love. After all, you could always get run over, suffer a broken heart, or fail.

An important part of the judge's evaluation consists in assessing this risk and figuring out the idea's chances for success and failure. Obviously, no judge wants to give his warrior an idea that's destined to fail. But he also realizes that nothing is foolproof. Like the "unsinkable" *Titanic,* every "100% sure thing" has an iceberg out there with its name on it.

So, what do you do? You realize that, as a judge, a large part of creative thinking is not being afraid to fail. Indeed, there is such a thing as being too conservative. As comedian Woody Allen put it, "If you're not failing every now and again it's a sign that you're not trying anything very innovative." To be sure, nobody wants to make a mistake, but if you do, try to realize the following benefits. First, you learn what doesn't work, and that gives you an opportunity to try new ideas and approaches.

As novelist James Joyce said, "A man's errors are his portals of discovery." Second, you learn that life goes on. Some people are so concerned about the possibility of failing that they never try anything new. And, third, if you're really afraid of failing, then you can use that as a motive to sharpen your judgment.

Unfortunately, many of us have learned that failing is a bad thing. In school you learn that:

Over 90% correct = "A"
Over 80% correct = "B"
Over 70% correct = "C"
Over 60% correct = "D"
And less than 60% fails.

With this kind of reward system, you learn that if you're wrong just 22% of the time, you get a "C." More importantly, you soon learn not to put yourself in situations where you might fail. The problem is that this leads to conservative thought and action patterns. These may be okay for much of what you do, but if you're trying to get a new idea into action, they're inappropriate. If there's only a 50% likelihood of success, but a 10 to 1 payback if successful, then your judge is a fool not to go with it—especially if he can motivate the warrior to perform.

A creative judge makes a distinction between *errors of commission* (errors you make when trying something new), and *errors of omission* (errors you make by doing nothing and perhaps losing an opportunity). Sometimes the person who doesn't do anything (and doesn't make any mistakes) is actually doing worse than the person who tries a few things and makes some mistakes. Edison knew 1800 ways not to build a light bulb. One of Madame Curie's failures was radium. Columbus thought he had discovered the East Indies. Freud had several big failures before he devised psychoanalysis. Rodgers and Hammerstein's first collaboration bombed so badly that they didn't get together again for years. As a matter of fact, the whole history of thought is filled with people who arrived at the "wrong" destinations.

Charles Kettering of General Motors, one of this century's great creative minds, had this to say on the value of learning to fail. "An inventor is simply a person who doesn't take his education too seriously. You see, from the time a person is six years old until he graduates from college he has to take three or four examinations a year. If he flunks once, he is out. But an inventor is almost always failing. He tries and fails maybe a thousand times. If he succeeds once then he's in. These two things are diametrically opposite. We often say that the biggest job we have is to teach a newly hired employee how to fail intelligently. We have to train him to experiment over and over and to keep on trying and failing until he learns what will work."

Exercise: What are the two biggest risks you've taken? Were you successful? What's a risk you took that didn't pay off? Did it improve your judgment?

Sometimes failure is simply the right idea at the wrong time. As technology observer Robert Gelber put it, "Never forget that the greatest idea at the wrong time is a loser. If you look at the "firsts" that were really seconds, they had timing in their favor. As with real estate, it's location, location, location; with ideas, it's timing, timing, timing."

Ask yourself: Is the timing right for this idea? What if I waited six months before implementing this? What advantages would be gained or lost? What if I did it six months ago?

What Assumptions Am I Making?

Exercise: Here's a chance for you to play Sherlock Holmes. You walk into a room and you find John and Mary lying dead on the floor. There's broken glass and water all around them. Your job is to figure out how they died.

Exercise: A woman goes into a store to buy something for her house. She asks about the price. The clerk replies, "The price of one is thirty-nine cents. The price of twenty-five is seventy-eight cents, and the price of one hundred and forty-four is a dollar and seventeen cents." What does the woman want to buy?

Assumptions are the mind's great success story. Because you're able to learn from past experience, you can anticipate what to expect in the various situations you encounter every day and respond in an appropriate fashion. If, for example, your boss has been grouchy the last seven Monday mornings, then you'll probably *assume* this coming Monday morning isn't the right time to hit him up for a raise. So, our assumptions help us get along in the world. The problem, for creative thinking, is that sometimes they channel our thinking in the wrong direction.

An exercise I like to do in my workshops involves making paper airplanes. I'll break the participants into teams and give each team fifty pieces of paper. Then I'll draw a line at the rear of the room. Each team has five minutes to see how many airplanes they can make that can fly past the line, and the one with the most is the winner. The most common approach is to fold the paper into the conventional paper airplane shape. The winning design, however, is to crumble the paper up into a ball and throw it. Invariably, it will "fly" past the line, and that's the only criterion that has to be satisfied in the exercise. Because many people already "know" what a paper airplane is supposed to look like, they place unnecessary restrictions on their thinking. Similarly, many people pre-judge a new idea and never give themselves an opportunity to ask the right questions.

Thomas Edison had a way around this. Whenever he was about to hire a new employee, he'd invite the candidate to lunch for a bowl of soup. He'd then watch the person very carefully to see if he salted his soup before tasting it. If he did, he wouldn't be offered the job. Edison felt that we have many assumptions built into our thinking by the everyday needs of living. He didn't want his people "salting their experience of life before tasting it."

How did you do with the Sherlock Holmes exercise at the beginning of this section? How did John and Mary die? Was it murder? Were they poisoned or shot to death? Perhaps they were stabbed with broken glass? Did a hurricane drown them? These explanations are plausible given the information with which you were provided and *assuming* that John and Mary are people. But let's suppose that they're not people. If you assume that they're fish, then you might come to a different judgment. Maybe the cat came in and knocked the fish bowl off the table.

Similarly, in the store problem, many people assume that 1, 25, and 144 represent the *quantity* of the objects the woman wishes to purchase. If, instead, you assume that they *are* the objects, then you'll figure out that the woman is buying house numbers and that's why "144" costs only three times as much as "1."

An elementary school teacher told me the following story about a colleague who had given her first graders a coloring assignment:

> The instructions said: "On this sheet of paper, you will find an outline of a house, trees, flowers, clouds and sky. Please color each with the appropriate colors."

> One of the students, Patty, put a lot of work into her drawing. When she got it back, she was surprised to find a big black "X" on it. She asked the teacher for an explanation. "I gave you an 'X' because you didn't follow instructions; grass is green, not gray and the sky should be blue, not yellow as you have drawn it. Why didn't you use the normal colors, Patty?"

> Patty answered, "Because that's how it looks to me when I get up early to watch the sunrise."

The teacher had assumed that there was only one right answer.

Your judge's bank of experience is a great resource. In certain situations, however, his ignorance can be just as valuable. Forgetting what you know—at the appropriate moment—can lead to good ideas. Without the ability to forget, your mind remains cluttered up with ready-made answers, and you never find the opportunity to ask the right questions. Remember: everyone has the ability to forget. The art is knowing when to use it. Indeed, novelist Henry Miller once said that his "forgettery" was just as important to his success as his memory.

Are My Assumptions Current?

It's important to make sure your assumptions are current. Since they're based on past experience, some of us make decisions like the driver who navigates his way down the freeway by looking in the rear view mirror. This approach works okay as long as what's up ahead is similar to where you've been, but if there's a curve up ahead you could be in for some trouble. Thus, your judge needs to be constantly updating his assumptions about the world.

There's a group of Russian immigrants in Los Angeles who have a tradition of celebrating New Year's Eve on the afternoon of December 30th. When they were asked why they brought in the new year thirty-six hours ahead of everyone else, one of them said, "When we were growing up in eastern Europe we didn't have much money, and it was cheaper to get a band on the afternoon of the 30th, rather than the next day. And that's how our tradition started." The curious thing is that now most of these people are financially well off, and they could easily afford entertainment on New Year's Eve, but they continue to celebrate on the afternoon of the 30th. The point: once an attitude or belief gets in place, it tends to live on even though the original reason for its generation no longer exists.

Every situation or problem has some of this "people celebrating early" for obsolete reasons. It could be the business forms you use. It could be the way you discipline your child. It could be the market opportunities you envision for a new product. It could be the age at which you decide to retire. Indeed, the 65 retirement age for many western nations is a prime example of this phenomenon. Back in the 1870's, German chancellor Otto von Bismarck arbitrarily set 65 as the age at which German civil servants could retire and receive a pension. This decision made good fiscal sense because average life expectancy then was considerably shorter than that. The problem is that life expectancy is currently much longer than 65, and yet that age is maintained even though prudent fiscal judgment might dictate otherwise.

To be effective, your judge should be looking for obsolete ideas. Indeed, this is one of the core ideas of creative thinking.

It's easy to come up with new ideas; the hard part is letting go of what worked for you two years ago, but will soon be out-of-date.

What's My Cultural Bias?

So much are the modes of excellence settled by time and place that men may be heard boasting in one street of that which they would anxiously conceal in another.
—Dr. Johnson, Lexicographer

Exercise: Quick now, which line is longer? Line AB or line BC?

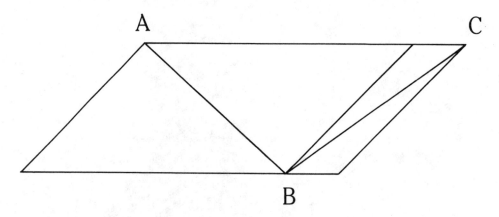

Sander Parallelogram

Exercise: Let's suppose that you're in the middle of a civil war. There are two armies fighting one another, a "red" army and a "white" army. Based solely on the associations you have for each color, which army would you give your allegiance to?

Sometimes we've inculcated our assumptions so deeply into our thinking that we're not even aware that they're guiding our judgment. The source of many of these deeply-engrained assumptions is our culture. There are many types of culture: truck driver's culture, managerial culture, jogger's culture, third grader's culture, and so on. What is self-evident in one may be foreign to another.

One way to understand how much our culture shapes our thinking is to leave it. For example, a few years ago when I was living in Germany, I went to a New Year's Eve party in Hamburg. It was a pleasant evening: good food, good drink, good people. About 10:30 someone brought out a big bowl of popcorn.

I thought, "Far out, I haven't had any popcorn in over six months," and I reached in and stuck a big handful in my mouth. Boy was I surprised: somebody had put sugar on the popcorn. I, of course, was expecting salt. As I learned that evening, in parts of northern Europe it's customary to put sugar on popcorn.

How did you do with the Sander Parallelogram? Which line did you judge to be longer? Most people answer line AB. If you measure them, however, you'll find that BC is actually 10% longer. Why don't we see this? One reason is that we live in a rectilinear world. There are right angles everywhere: on windows, doors, books, sheets of paper. Rarely, however, do you see these right angles straight on. You usually *see* them as parallelograms. But since you *know* they're rectangles you make a mental adjustment and *think* of them as right angles. That's the reason for the illusion. When this same exercise is shown to people living in "round" worlds (rural Uganda), they say that BC is longer.

How did you answer the civil war problem? If you said you'd support the "white" army, you're with the majority. For most of us, white brings to mind such positive ideas as "purity," "beauty," "chastity," and "justice;" and red conjures up "danger," "blood," and "communism." Well, this situation—a Red army fighting a White army—actually happened in Russia during their civil war. At the beginning of the conflict, the White army had a material superiority over the Red one, but they went on to lose. There were many reasons for their defeat, but one had to do with the color associations most Russians have with red and white. Red is synonymous with "beauty," "poppies blooming in the springtime," and the "regeneration of life" while white brings up images of "cold," "snow," "exile," "Siberia," and other negative experiences.

My favorite example of cultural confusion is psychologist Paul Watzlawick's description of what happened when American soldiers dated Englishwomen during World War II. The problem was that both the men and the women accused each other of being sexually aggressive. What caused this? The answer: confused cues. Anthropologists say that every culture has a courtship procedure consisting of approximately thirty steps beginning with first eye contact on through to the consummation of the relationship. The interesting thing is that not every culture has these steps in the same place. In the North American pattern, kissing is about #5—it's a friendly way of getting the relationship started. In pre World War II England, however, kissing was about step #25—it was considered a highly erotic activity. Now imagine what would happen when an American GI and an Englishwoman would get together. They'd go out, have a date or two, and then the soldier would think, "I'll give her a kiss to get this relationship going." He kisses her and she's astounded. She thinks, "This isn't supposed to happen until step #25." Furthermore, she feels like she's just been cheated out of 20 steps in the courtship process. But now she must make a decision: either break off the relationship because it's gone too far too fast, or get ready for intercourse since it's only five steps away. From the man's point of view, the situation is equally confusing: she acts either like a woman in hysteria or a nymphomaniac.

My point with these exercises and stories is that if life is a game, each culture makes different rules. Blindly following them can cause your judge to make poor decisions.

What's Clouding My Thinking?

Some people have built-in filters that screen
out the boos and amplify the hurrahs.
Those are the people who
never know when they're in trouble.
—Tommy Davis, Venture Capitalist

I tell you Wellington is a bad general,
the English are bad soldiers; we will
settle this matter by lunch time.
—Napoleon Bonaparte, at breakfast with his generals
on the morning of the Battle of Waterloo.

Nothing clouds your judge's mind like dogma. This dogma can come from an outside authority or it can be self-generated from one's past successes. Here are some examples.

None other than Plato himself dictated that the circle was the perfect form for celestial movement, and for the next two thousand years, astronomers said that planetary orbits were circular—even though their observations didn't quite jibe with that. Even Copernicus used circles in his heliocentric model of the universe. Only after much soul-searching did Kepler use the ellipse to describe the heavenly paths.

Joseph Semmelweiss, the 19th century Hungarian physician, felt that doctors could reduce disease by washing their hands in chlorinated lime water before inspecting their patients. His colleagues—because they thought that doctors were close to God—strongy resented his suggestion that they were "carrying death around on their hands," and denounced him. The later discovery of bacteria proved Semmelweiss correct.

Having a big success with one set of assumptions can easily create a dogmatic outlook. Edison founded the electricity supply industry using direct current (DC). This prevented him from seeing both the benefits of alternating current (AC) and that the future of the industry lay with that type of current.

Henry Ford had been successful making cars available in only one color ("Any color you want as long as it's black"). He believed that he had a formula that worked, and he didn't want to change it. This prevented him from seeing the rise of a post World War I consumer class that wanted a variety of styles and colors from which to choose. As a result, Ford lost market share to General Motors.

In order to make good decisions, your judge should avoid falling in love with ideas—especially those that have brought him success in the past.

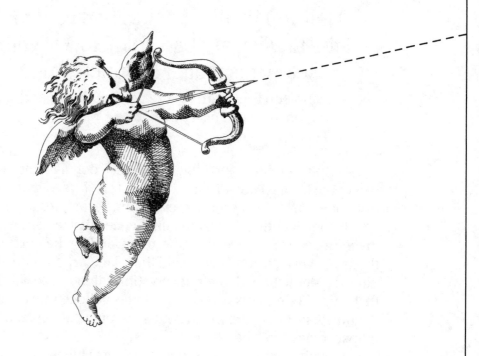

Exercise: What ideas are you in love with that might prevent you from seeing things clearly?

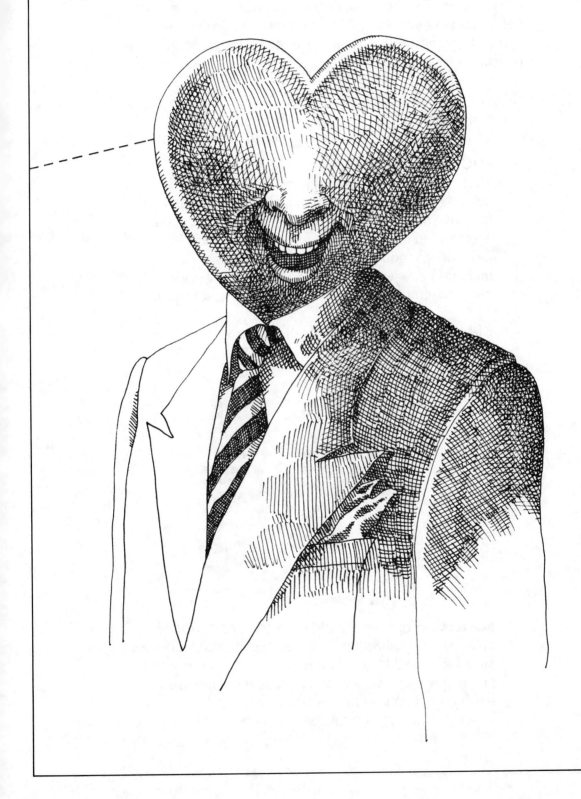

Bring In The Fool

Occasionally, the judge needs to let his stupid monitor down and be a little crazy. An exercise I highly recommend any judge to play is the "Fools and the Rules." In it you roast your basic beliefs and assumptions. By doing so, you may discover that some of your assumptions are obsolete or dogmatic, and thus may be clouding your thinking. At the very least, it's a lot of fun.

Here are some examples:

RULE: We should have "excellence in management."

FOOL: On the contrary, we need mediocre managers. That would help solve the unemployment problem because a run-of-the-mill manager needs more people to get the job done than an excellent one. Poor managers would drive down the price of the stock so that more people could afford it. Bad management also increases efficiency. In order to get anything done, the other systems have to be functioning extremely well.

RULE: Our policy is: no alcohol at work.

FOOL: Of course we should have drinking at work. It's an incentive to show up. Not only that, it would reduce stress and would lead to more honest communications. Our fellow employees would look better. There'd be fewer complaints about low pay. It would cut down on absenteeism—you could come to work hung over. It would improve communications; you'd tell your manager exactly what you thought. It would save on heating costs in the winter and would encourage car pooling. It would decrease job dissatisfaction; if you had a bad job, you wouldn't know it. Finally, it would eliminate vacation: people would rather go to work.

Exercise: Pick one of your basic beliefs and roast it.

Making The Decision

If you spend too much time warming up, you'll miss the race. If you don't warm up at all, you may not finish the race.
—Grant Heidrich, Runner

The most important thing your judge must do is make a decision. If he doesn't, he'll stymie the creative process. Sometimes you have only a few seconds to evaluate a situation. Sometimes you have six months. Sometimes you have incomplete information. Sometimes you have too much. That's the real world. You've got to decide what to do with the idea: go or no-go.

Tip: Ethernet inventor Bob Metcalfe put it well when he said, "Don't let your search for the great idea blind you to the merely good or promising idea. Often that's all the warrior needs. If it's a great idea so much the better. But if you reject everything except the very best, you may leave your warrior with nothing to fight for." Stanford University president Donald Kennedy has similar feelings: "A lot of disappointed people have been left standing on the street corner waiting for the bus marked 'Perfection'."

Another Tip: Reason is important in decision-making, but don't ignore your gut. One person told me, "If I get an idea, and it won't go away then I have to do it. This takes a fair amount of self-trust, but I find that it works." Another said, "If I have three ideas and I feel a great amount of passion for one of them, then that's the one I'll spend my time on."

Summary

The judge performs the evaluation function of the creative process. When you adopt this role, you decide what to do with the idea: implement it, modify it, or discard it completely. In carrying out this task, you should recognize imperfections in the new idea without overstating them. You should also be open to interesting possibilities and use your imagination to develop these without losing your sense of reality and perspective.

There's an art to being a judge. On the one hand, you have to be critical enough to insure that you give the warrior an idea worth fighting for; on the other, you have to be open enough so as not to stifle your artist. In addition, you need to figure out which decisions require a short amount of time and which ones demand a lot of careful study. If you don't, you may lose opportunities because you weren't fast enough, or make bad decisions because you didn't do all your homework.

If there's a role that people get stuck in more than any other, it's the judge. There are three main reasons for this. First, there's a lot of crap, hype and pretense in the world and you need your judge to cut through it. Second, it's the role that takes the least amount of energy. It's easier to criticize than to explore, transform, or act. And, third, it's the role that has the least amount of risk. Your explorer could get lost, your artist could get rejected, and your warrior could get wounded. Remember, however, that the judge neither creates nor implements, and if you spend all of your time in this role, you won't get much accomplished.

Finally, no judge is perfect. After all, we've all known great ideas that proved to be mediocre...and mediocre ideas that turned out to be great.

The Judge's Scales

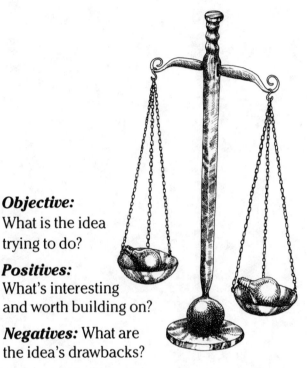

Objective:
What is the idea
trying to do?

Positives:
What's interesting
and worth building on?

Negatives: What are
the idea's drawbacks?

Probability: What are its chances of success?

Downside: If it fails, what can be salvaged?

Ripeness: Is the timing right for this idea?

Deadline: How long do you have to make your decision?

Bias: What assumptions are you making?

Currency: Are these assumptions still valid?

Blind Spot: What assumptions are you making that you're not
even aware of?

Arrogance: Have you been successful with similar ideas in the
past? If so, could this success prevent you from seeing pitfalls in
the idea?

Humor: What would the fool say about the idea?

Verdict: What's your decision?

The Warrior

Your role for carrying your idea into action

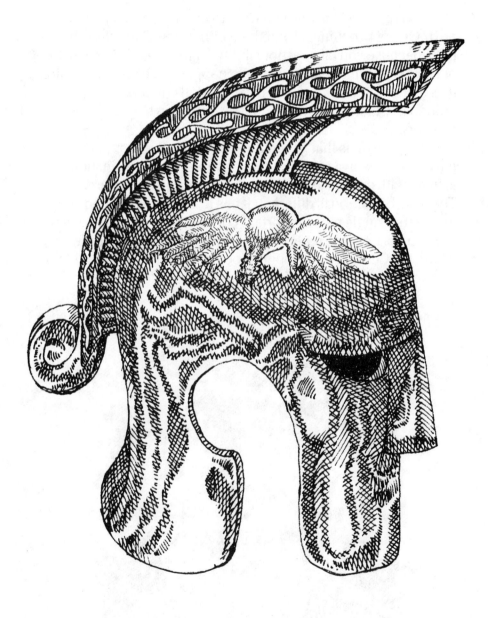

Moving From "What If" To "What Is"

Try? There is no try.
There is only do or not do.

—Yoda, in *The Empire Strikes Back*

You have an idea that you want to implement. What happens next? One of two things: something or nothing. *Something* happens because you take responsibility for the idea and do what's necessary to implement it. *Nothing* happens because something gets in the way, and you don't have the skills or energy to get around it. Unfortunately, many ideas end up in the second category.

The reason is that generating the idea is the easy part; making it a reality is another story. The world of imagination is filled with endless possibilities and boundless resources. The world of action is different. It has finite resources and still less of that single most important commodity—time. Thus, few ideas cross from the realm of the "what if" to the world of "what is." As the German philosopher Goethe put it, "To put your ideas into action is the most difficult thing in the world."

Two basic rules of life are:

1) Change Is Inevitable
2) Everybody Resists Change

As a matter of fact, much of the world has its defenses up to keep new ideas out. Think for a moment of all the walls, screens, and boundaries that exist: cell walls that prevent foreign proteins from entering your body; secretaries who screen telephone calls for their bosses; the body language you use in an elevator to prevent strange people from starting conversations with you.

Thus, you'll probably have to fight to get your idea implemented. Your role for doing this is your warrior. As a warrior, you're part general and part foot-soldier. You develop the strategy and put your plan together. You also have the discipline to slog it out in the trenches and the passion to keep on going when things get tough. In short, when you adopt this role, you take responsibility for making your idea a reality.

Who is a warrior? It's Alexander the Great smashing the Persians at the Granicus River and Joan of Arc breaking the siege of Orleans. It's Susan B. Anthony leading the women's suffrage movement in the United States, and Mahatma Gandhi working to bring independence to India. It's a salesman who makes a hard-to-reach quota because he doesn't mind being told "no" 90% of the time and continues to prospect for customers. It's your neighbor down the street who champions a local zoning change and convinces the city council to accept it. It's an office worker who figures out how to save 10% on copying costs and gets his department to change its rules. Whether your battlefield is the marketplace in which you compete for new clients for your accounting firm, or the classroom in which you're taking a final exam, you—as a creative thinker—need to think like a warrior when you carry an idea into action.

Here's a personal example. Several years ago, I wanted to put on a conference that would draw together the world's top high technology innovators to talk about the future of their industry. I wanted it to be a first-class affair. I wanted it to be thought-provoking. And, of course, I wanted it to be well-attended in order to earn a profit. What did I do? I put together my plan. I scheduled a date at a fine hotel. I found out what the major issues were in the industry and who people wanted to hear. I got several important people to commit to the idea to give it credibility. One by one I lined up my speakers. Some wouldn't return my phone calls. I made friends with their secretaries. I found out if any of my friends knew them and could tell them what a fine job I'd do. After a lot of work, I got my program together.

Now, the real fun started: I had to promote the conference. After all, I didn't want the world's leading innovators showing up for a room full of empty chairs. So I put together a brochure. But not just any brochure. No, this had to be eye-catching so that it wouldn't be thrown away unopened. I got the best graphic designer I could and gave him the mind-popping copy I'd written. I did a mailing. I advertised in the *Wall Street Journal.* And people started to sign up. Now I had to think about the show itself. I wanted to make it interesting so that the audience would demand that I do it again in six months. I got the best conference planner I could find to help me with the logistics. I got a three-piece jazz band to play at seven in the morning. I used old television commercials to introduce the speakers and to spice up the program. I got venture capital firms to sponsor the wine-reception. The conference was a big success. My explorer, artist, and judge helped to create the idea. My warrior made it happen.

What follows are eight basic strategies your warrior can use to reach his goal.

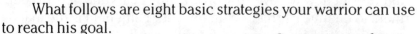

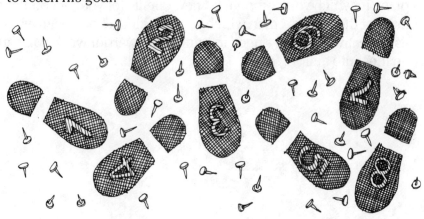

Put Your Plan Together

You can walk up to people on the street and ask them if they want to be rich and 99% will tell you, "Sure I want to be rich." But are they willing to do what's necessary to be successful? Not many are.

—Arthur Rock, Venture Capitalist

What's your objective? What is it that you want to accomplish? Can you state it simply in a sentence or two? Can you draw a picture of it? Can you visualize yourself reaching your objective?

What's your plan? How do you intend to get from here to there? What are the five or ten most important things you'll have to do to reach your objective? Which are the most crucial? Which are less important? Which can you do today? Which are dependent on what you do tomorrow? You'll probably have many smaller battles to fight on the way to reaching your objective. Do you have a strategy?

How do you expect to deal with the obstacles in your path? Brute force? Finesse? Surprise? Diplomacy? Dogged persistence?

What are your resources? Do you have a war chest? Who are your allies? Who are five people who can help you reach your objective? Who are your models? Who has done a similar thing to what you want to accomplish? What can you learn from them?

Think how you'll sell your idea.

Stay focused on your objective. If you're trying to do fifty other things at the same time, you can't expect to do a good job on this one. Figure out which battles are worth fighting, and which ones are a waste of energy.

Commit yourself to being successful. Consider the sacrifices you'll need to make. Consider the consequences of failing. Don't be satisfied unless you've given it your best shot.

Put A Fire in Your Belly

The basic difference between an ordinary man and a warrior is that a warrior takes everything as a challenge while an ordinary man takes everything either as a blessing or a curse.

—Carlos Castaneda, Anthropologist

Exercise: What motivates you to get your idea into action? What fires you up?

- ☐ Personal expression
- ☐ Money
- ☐ Survival
- ☐ Recognition
- ☐ Fun and enjoyment
- ☐ Boredom
- ☐ Fear of failure
- ☐ Deadlines
- ☐ Dissatisfaction

All of these stoke our creative fires. One very compelling motive is that things are changing quickly. What worked last year may not be the best way to solve this year's problems or take advantage of next year's opportunities. Thus, survival means implementing your new ideas.

Another motivator is dissatisfaction. I once met an inventor who spent sixteen hours a day practicing his craft. When I asked him why he spent so much time pursuing his ideas, he replied, "Because I'm dissatisfied with everything as it currently exists in its present form." On a similar note, British humorist Christopher Morley once remarked that, "High heels were invented by a woman who had been kissed on the forehead."

How about deadlines? Commercial jingle writer Steve Karmen once remarked, "The ultimate inspiration is the deadline. That's when you have to do what needs to be done." In a like vein, entertainment entrepreneur Nolan Bushnell has theorized that what has made American business successful is the "Trade Show" phenomenon. As he puts it, "The fact that twice a year the creative talent of this country is working until midnight to get something ready for a trade show is very good for the economy. Without this kind of pressure, things would turn to mashed potatoes."

Another driving motive is having passion for your idea. Several entrepreneurs have told me, "You make what you want for yourself. It's this desire that propels you over any obstacle that stands in the way of reaching your objective."

What puts a fire in your belly? Whatever it is, use it to spur yourself into action.

Put A Lion In Your Heart

If the creator had a purpose in equipping us with a neck, he surely would have meant for us to stick it out.

—Arthur Koestler, Student of Human Nature

Courage is the first of human qualities because it is the quality which guarantees the others.

—Aristotle, Philosopher

A new idea is different by nature—it's off the beaten path—and it takes courage to risk failure or rejection. For example, how do you know that your brilliant insight isn't going to lead you into a blind alley, make you look stupid, cost you money, or worse? You don't. Thus, a crucial element of creative thinking is having the courage to take a risk.

Exercise: What gives you courage to try a new idea?

- ☐ Having a well-thought out plan of attack
- ☐ Past success
- ☐ Big potential payoff
- ☐ Encouragement from other people
- ☐ Belief in yourself
- ☐ Faith in the idea
- ☐ Having a "plan B"
- ☐ Having no other alternative

What is courage? The dictionary says something along the lines of "the mental strength to venture, persevere, and withstand danger, fear, or difficulty." I think a better definition comes from its etymology. Courage comes from the Old French word *cuer* and the Latin word *cor,* both of which mean "heart." So, having courage means putting your heart into your effort!

Tip: Everyone has a "risk muscle." You keep it in shape by trying new things. If you don't, it atrophies. Make a point of using it at least once a day.

Get Going

If you're putting off something you've been meaning to do, what are you waiting for? Always wanted to play the banjo? Start taking lessons. Dreamt about visiting Greek Islands? Call a travel agent. Hate your bathroom wallpaper? Scrape it off and paint. Feel better if you've exercised? Start jogging. Love the taste of home-grown tomatoes? Plant your own. Angry about the potholes in your street? Go to your town meetings. Whatever you've been putting off, do it *now.* Tomorrow may be too late.

—Harry Gray, Business Executive

Whatever it is you need to do first, do it. Get going. Don't make negative assumptions about the outcome. That's for your judge to worry about.

Sharpen your sword. Develop the skills that will enable you to implement your idea. If it means learning how to sell, then do it. If it means learning some technical skills then do that. If it means developing people skills, then do that.

Put yourself in a position to achieve your objective. If you want to be a singer, don't think about *wanting to be* a singer, go sing. Sing in the shower. Sing for your friends. Join the choir. Sing for free. Go do it.

Get Rid Of Your Excuses

You can't hit a home run unless you step up to the plate. You can't catch fish unless you put your line in the water. You can't reach your goals it you don't try.

—Kathy Seligman, Journalist

To know and not to do is not to know.

—Saying on Wall Street

Exercise: What was the last good idea you had that you didn't execute? What reasons did you have?

- ☐ "I didn't have the time."
- ☐ "I didn't know what to do next."
- ☐ "I couldn't sell it."
- ☐ "I didn't get any support."
- ☐ "I didn't have the resources."
- ☐ "I was afraid of failing."
- ☐ "I wasn't really committed."

These are all valid reasons. But valid or not, they're the excuses that prevent you from getting your ideas into action. It's your warrior's job to eliminate these excuses.

The Spanish explorer Cortez knew all about this. When he landed at Veracruz in the sixteenth century, the first thing he did after unloading his equipment was to burn his ships. He then gave his men a pep talk. "Men," he told them, "you can either fight or you can die." What he did by burning the ships was to eliminate a third alternative—namely turning tail and going back to Spain. Cortez knew this could have been a potential excuse to lose, and burning the ships gave his men a powerful motive to win. Thus, you have to make a commitment to your idea; you have to learn to "burn your ships" by convincing yourself that you cannot turn back.

A similar situation happened to me several years ago as a Masters swimmer. The night before my first national competition at Mission Viejo, I was talking with my teammates about the fact that this was our first big meet in over a decade since competing in college. One of them, a breaststroker, decided to shave his legs in order to reduce resistance. As we talked about it, I also decided to shave my legs to give myself a psychological advantage for my most important race, the 500 yard freestyle. The 500 is about a five minute race. Sometimes I go out too hard, get tired at 400 yards, and then die. I promised myself that evening that I would hang in there no matter what. The next day, I swam a great race and finished sixth in the country, defeating a former Olympic gold medal winner in the process. I realized that by shaving my legs, I had eliminated any excuses for a poor performance. If I had done poorly and said, "Well, I really wasn't up for the race," I never would have been able to answer the question, "Why did you shave your legs?"

An engineer told me the following story about his repeated attempts to quit smoking. It seemed that every time he stopped, he'd get constipated within a few days. After a week of constipation, he'd use this as an excuse to resume smoking. He went through this cycle of quitting smoking, getting constipated, and resuming smoking a number of times. Finally, he realized that he needed to take charge and eliminate his excuse. He went to the grocery store and bought a twenty-five pound bag of prunes and then quit smoking again. Then every time he desired a cigarette, he popped a prune. Within several weeks, he had solved both of his problems.

Exercise: What are three factors that will make it difficult for you to reach your goal? Are you going to use these as "reasons"—excuses—not to reach your goal?

Strengthen Your Shield

A thick skin is a gift from God.

—Konrad Adenauer, Father of Post WWII Germany

If you can't stand the heat, get out of the kitchen.

—Harry Truman, 33rd President
of the United States

Exercise: How do you react to criticism?

☐ "It's part of the game. If you're going to be doing new things, you've got to expect some people to take a shot at you because they feel threatened or don't understand."

☐ "If I think I'm going to get criticized, I'm hesitant to try new things."

New ideas can be threatening. By definition, they question existing rules, hierarchies, and assumptions. When Stravinsky first presented his *Rite of Spring* ballet, he was met with a rioting audience. When Kepler correctly solved the orbital problem of the planets using ellipses rather than circles, he was denounced. When early microcomputer developers tried to sell their ideas to the larger established companies in the 1970's, they were laughed at. As educator Roy Blitzer put it:

The only person who likes change is a wet baby.

Negative reaction to new ideas isn't a bad thing. Because many new ideas aren't any good (some people's judges aren't functioning at full gavel), they can be a drain on resources, and a negative reception can flush them away. In addition, if everyone went along with every new idea that came along, things would be in chaos.

The 1951 British film, *The Man in the White Suit,* provides a good illustration of this. In it, Alec Guiness plays Sid, a polymer engineer who has created an indestructible fiber that never needs cleaning. Sounds like a boon to mankind, right? Well, the owners of the mills don't want the fiber because it would knock the bottom out of the textile markets. Labor's not hot for it either because it would eliminate jobs. Here's a scene in which Sid shares his discovery with a co-worker.

Sid: We're just going to announce my new fiber to the press.

Worker (reading Sid's press release aloud): "It never gets dirty and never wears out."

Sid: That's right.

Worker: And you think management will go along with it?

Sid: Yes.

Worker: You're not even born yet. What do you think happened to all the other things? The razor blade that never gets blunt? The car that runs on water with a pinch of something in it? They'll never let your stuff on the market in a million years.

Sid: It's not like that.

Worker: If this stuff never wears out, we'll only have one lot of it to make. That's lovely, six months' work and every mill in the country will be closed. Something's got to be done about it.

The rest of the movie has both the mill owners and the workers chasing Sid so they can get rid of his fiber. When they finally corner him, they're relieved to discover that his white suit of wonder fiber is falling apart, and that the fiber isn't indestructible after all.

The point is many people will take a shot at your idea. You'll hear comments like:

It's too radical.

That's contrary to policy.

It won't work in our industry.

Can you guarantee that it will work?

It worries our lawyers.

It would be impractical.

We could never market that.

We don't have the time.

Maybe they're right. Maybe your idea is half-baked. Indeed, one of the best things you can receive is good criticism. However, often times people use idea killers because they feel threatened by your idea and want to shoot it down. Thus, it's important to remember that idea killers are generally used indiscriminately, and if someone starts using one on your idea, recognize it for what it is.

Sell, Sell, Sell

It's not creative unless it sells.

—Motto of Benton & Bowles Advertising Agency

Exercise: Several years ago, the following advertisement appeared in the *Wall Street Journal*.

THE STRESS SYNDROME

Something is happening in offices and factories. In restaurants and hospitals. In banks and supermarkets.

It's stress. And it's partly caused by noise—all kinds of noise—from typewriter bells to conversation.

Studies show that stress debilitates and retards performance. It makes us vulnerable.

You can do something about the stress syndrome....

The ad continues by telling the reader how he can solve his stress problem. Can you guess what the product is?

Many ideas require the investment of other people's time, resources, or commitment. Your warrior should be thinking, "What is there about my idea that will attract people's interest to it? What will make this idea sell?"

Does your warrior think like a salesman? He'd better. Living in a market economy requires you to be constantly selling ideas: to your boss, to your peers, to your subordinates, and to your spouse. If you can't sell your ideas, then you may have some trouble. I've met many people with great ideas who couldn't get them implemented because they couldn't sell them. Indeed, sometimes it takes as much creativity to figure how to sell your idea as it does to come up with the idea in the first place.

One of my favorite ways to sell is to emphasize not the idea or the product itself, but rather:

The product of the product.

By selling "the product of the product," you put the idea in a context that the potential buyer knows and understands. Here are some examples. In the early 1960's, a leading hardware manufacturer introduced a new line of drills into the marketplace. These were well-engineered drills, but when they hit the market they just didn't sell. The company decided to do some market research and found out that most potential drill purchasers don't think in terms of "drills," but rather "holes"—which is their "product of the product." They then successfully re-positioned their product to emphasize the drills' "hole-creating" power.

Another example is Charles Revson, one of the founders of Revlon. At a cocktail party in the early 1970's a lady asked him what his product was. Revson replied, "My dear lady, on the factory floors, our product is cosmetics, but in the department stores, our product is *hope.*"

How did you do with the "stress syndrome" exercise? What did you think the product was? Quieter office machinery? Acoustical ceiling tile? White-noise generators? Stress management consultants? A travel agency? A pharmaceutical company? These are all good guesses. The ad, however, was sponsored by Muzak™ background music. If you continue to read the copy, it says:

> With Muzak, you can create an environment that surrounds and pleases. It smooths out monotony, relaxes patients, makes people feel better about their meals, and sharpens concentration.

In a word, Muzak promises to make people more *productive.* That's a savvy marketing approach. When some people think of Muzak, they put it in the same context as "plastic flowers" and "being put on hold." By emphasizing the product of their product, the Muzak people have positioned themselves to be in the "stress reduction" and "productivity" businesses.

One other point about selling the product of the product: there are many products of the product. If you're talking to a housewife, it's one thing, to an engineer, another, to a farmer still another.

Tip: Think about selling your idea. What is its "product of your product?" What opportunities does it create for other people?

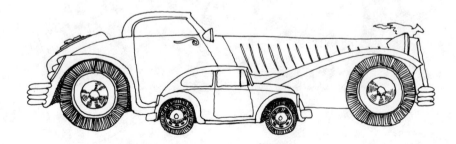

Exercise: Here's a test to help you to think like a marketer. My friend, Bryan Mattimore, is an extraordinary inventor. However, he can't remember the names assigned by his advertising agency to his eight most recent inventions. Can you help Bryan out? Match each product name with its description.

Product Name

1) *On-Cue*
Puts your opponent in your back (and side) pocket!

2) *Two Heads Are Better Than One*
Let someone else learn things for you!

3) *Stop! In The Name of Love*
Makes it *his* responsibility too!

4) *The Parking Plate*
You no longer need to play "bumper cars" getting in those tight spaces.

5) *Only The Strong Survive*
When *you* want to last as long as your clothes do.

6) *Dream Makers*
Your "night life" need never stop

7) *The Whiff-le Ball*
With 10,000 smells to choose from, you'll have a ball!

8) *The Swimmer's Ear*
That hammerhead'll never catch you with your harpoon down again!

Product Description

A) Sleeper's videos

B) Bullet-proof fashions

C) Spherical odor-generating device

D) Digital-sighting pool stick

E) Underwater hearing aid

F) Brain-to-brain information transferrer

G) Distance-measuring license plate

H) The male "pill"

Be Persistent

Let us run with perseverance
the race that is set before us.
—Hebrews 12:1

When down in the mouth,
remember Jonah—he came out all right.
—Thomas Edison, Inventor

Be prepared to strike quickly to reach your goal. However, also be prepared for a long campaign. Sometimes as much as eighty percent of the creative process consists in doggedly plodding toward your objective.

You're likely to get knocked down a few times along the way. If that happens, get up. Otherwise you'll end up with footprints on your back. Everyone has setbacks. People don't return your phone calls. Your brochure gets printed on the wrong paper. Your souffle falls. It rains on your parade. The little sales gimmicks you try don't work. When something goes wrong, your warrior should find out why and then press on.

Indeed, a recent survey of venture capitalists showed that the characteristic they look for most often when investing in an entrepreneur is the latter's "ability to sustain an intense effort." (This was rated more highly than "market familiarity," "demonstrated past leadership," and "ability to take a risk.")

Michelangelo had to endure seven years lying on his back on a scaffold to paint the Sistine Chapel. Vladimir Lenin spent thirty years preparing for his revolution. Inventor Chester Carlson pounded the streets for years before he could find backers for his "Xerox" photocopying process. Novelist James Michener was turned down a number of times before he got his first work, *Tales of the South Pacific*, published. Marathoner Joan Benoit underwent knee surgery only seventeen days before the U.S. Olympic Trials, but her determination enabled her not only to make the team, but also to win the first ever Olympic gold medal in her event. As Winston Churchill put it when asked to describe the most important lesson life had taught him, "Never give up, never give up, never ever give up."

Someone once gave me the following advice which expresses this point quite well.

Nothing in the world can take the place of persistence.

Talent will not; nothing is more common than unsuccessful men with talent.

Genius will not; unrewarded genius is almost a proverb.

Education will not; the world is full of educated derelicts.

Persistence and determination alone are omnipotent.

Warning: If you don't execute your ideas, they die.

Summary

The warrior is your role for carrying an idea from the world of "what if" to the world of action. When you adopt this role, not only do you take responsibility for making the idea a reality, you also provide the payoff for the whole creative process. That's because the creative process is not a series of linear steps but an on-going cycle. It is the warrior who completes the loop and gives feedback to the other roles about what works, what doesn't, and what has possibilities.

The two greatest enemies of action are fear and lack of confidence. Your most important weapon to combat these is in your head. It's your belief that you can make it happen. As Henry Ford put it, "Whether you think you can or can't, you're right." With a can-do attitude, you give yourself courage, and eliminate the self-doubt and fear of failure that may prevent you from reaching your objective.

Finally, remember the words of Carl Ally:

Either you let your life slip away by
not doing the things you want to do, or
you get up and do them.

The Warrior's Battle Cry

Be bold. What qualities do you have that will enable you to implement your idea?

Put together your plan. What's your strategy to reach your objective?

Put a fire in your belly. What motivates you to reach your goal?

Put a lion in your heart. What are you willing to sacrifice? What are the consequences of failure?

Get going. What excuses may prevent you from getting started?

Capitalize on your resources. Who are five people who can help you realize your idea?

Sharpen your sword. What skills can you develop to implement your idea?

Know what you're selling. What is your idea's "product of the product?"

Strengthen your shield. What type of criticism do you expect to receive? How can you deflect it?

Follow through. What obstacles might get in the way? How will you get around them?

Use your energy wisely. What are some needless battles you can avoid?

Get up when you get knocked down. How persistent are you?

Savor your victories and learn from your defeats. What did you accomplish? What did you learn?

Summing Up

Summing Up

In this book, we have looked at the four roles of the creative process. To review them:

Your explorer is your role for searching for the materials with which to make new ideas.

Your artist is your imaginative, playful role. His job is to take the materials the explorer has collected and transform them into original new ideas.

Your judge is your evaluative role. His job is to examine what the artist has created and then decide what to do with it: implement it, modify it, or discard it.

Your warrior is your "doer." His role is to take the ideas the judge has deemed worthy and do what's necessary to implement them.

Sometimes you'll go through all four roles in just a short period. Suppose you're in an important meeting and someone asks you a difficult question. Your explorer will comb through your mind looking for facts and information that have a bearing on the question. Your artist will mold these into an answer. Your judge will decide if the answer is appropriate. And, your warrior will confidently deliver the response.

Sometimes you may spend a long time in each of the roles. Suppose you're developing a new product. You may spend months as an explorer doing market research. You may spend an equal amount of time as an artist and a judge in the course of developing and refining the concept. And finally, you may spend a year or more clearing the various hurdles that are part of manufacturing the product and getting it to market.

Take a look at your own creative team. How adventurous is your explorer? How off-the-wall is your artist? How reliable is your judge? How persistent is your warrior? I've got one friend who's a competent explorer, an outstanding artist, an adequate judge, and a lousy warrior. As a result, he comes up with wonderful ideas that never go anywhere. I've got another friend who's mediocre—but competent—for the first three roles, and then a ferocious warrior. As a result, she implements a lot of moderately innovative ideas. I have a third friend who has a strong artist, a weak judge, and a tremendous warrior. As you might expect, a lot of terrific and terrible ideas get put into action.

Thus, being able to adopt all four roles is vital to having a dynamic creative process. As I pointed out earlier, if you're significantly weak in one or more of the roles, then you will have some problems. If your explorer isn't getting off the beaten path, you won't have any new information to draw upon. If your artist doesn't use his imagination, your ideas won't be very original. If your judge isn't discerning enough, you may be making the wrong call. And if your warrior isn't forceful enough, you may not be able to get over the obstacles that stand in the way of making your idea a reality.

Thus, it's important to get and keep all of your roles in good shape. It's also important to know when it's appropriate to adopt each one. As with most things in life, timing is essential. Wearing a bathing suit to the beach makes sense. Wearing a bathing suit to meet the President makes the Secret Service uneasy. Similarly, adopting a role at the wrong time can be counterproductive.

Depending on which role you use, any given situation can produce a variety of different results. For example, let's suppose you go camping in a wilderness area. Your explorer will want to do such things as look for wildflowers and go hiking to the waterfalls. Your artist will want to make up stories about the stars, and cook a special stew. Your judge will be concerned about the weather and any dangerous animals. Your warrior will be ready for anything that might come up.

It's also important to be flexible in moving from role to role. At any given time, you're probably working on a number of different projects. You may go from being a judge on where to invest your money to being a warrior in selling an idea to your boss to being an artist in landscaping your back yard. Thus, you're not only shifting in and out of various roles for each project but usually shifting between roles from project to project. You need to make sure that you don't get stuck in the role you just left.

Enjoy the theater of your mind!

Jack's Return Visit To The Idea Doctor

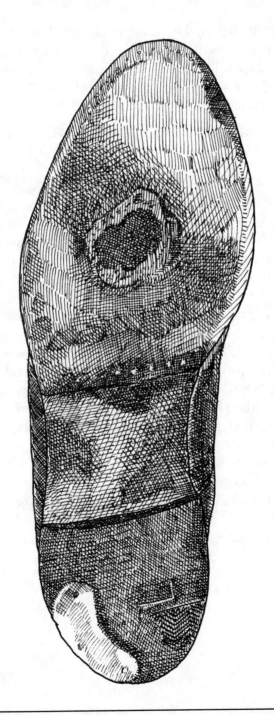

The Return Visit to the Idea Doctor

Getting ideas is like shaving:
if you don't do it every day, you're a bum.
—Alex Kroll, Advertising Executive

A month after he'd received his kick in the seat of the pants, Jack returned to see the idea doctor. "That kick sure got my attention," Jack told him. "I've gone exploring in new places. I've created new things. My judgment is better. And I've been more persistent in pursuing my goals."

"That's great," said the idea doctor. "What can I do for you today?"

"Well, I'm afraid that the kick may wear off. How can I make sure that I don't need one again?"

The idea doctor looked at him and said, "Let me tell you a story, Jack. Several years ago, a frozen-fish processor was having trouble getting repeat sales of its new line of frozen fish. The president looked into the matter and found that his customers didn't reorder because the fish tasted 'flat.' He tried just about every method of keeping the fish fresh including holding them live in tanks until right before they could be processed. But nothing worked. He'd about run out of ideas when an expert on the natural history of fish happened by. The man offered one comment: 'Why don't you put a predator in there with them?' This idea worked like a charm. The fish kept moving to avoid being consumed, and as a result, they retained their vitality. There was some loss but it was more than offset by a thriving market. What the predator did was force the fish to pay attention to what was going on around them."

The idea doctor went on, "I'm going to give you something that will help you pay attention to your thinking." At this point, he went to his safe, opened it, and gave Jack a picture.

"This is your thought monitor," the idea doctor said. "It's a picture of the shoe I used to give you a kick in the seat of the pants. When you look at it, I want it to trigger these questions in your mind:

Am I getting lazy?
Am I too busy?
Am I becoming arrogant?
Am I getting timid?

If you answer 'yes' to any one of them, that's your warning to kick that attitude. For example, if you think you're being lazy, then set a tight deadline for yourself to accomplish some specific objective. If you find that you're too busy, then clear out a day or two to take a look at the big picture and put things in perspective. If you're getting arrogant, then imagine what you'd do if the situation you're feeling so smug about ceased to exist. And if you're feeling timid, then exercise your risk muscle and put yourself in a situation that will give you a better sense of who you are.

"Use this thought monitor once a day and you won't have to worry about getting your ends reversed. What's more, your thinking will be vital and you'll continue to do many creative things."

Jack took the picture of the shoe home with him and hung it up where he could see it every morning as he shaved. He had learned that in the long run, he had to be the one to give himself the kick. And he's been doing creative things ever since.

Dear reader: here is your picture. Cut it out, color it, and put it where it will do the most good.

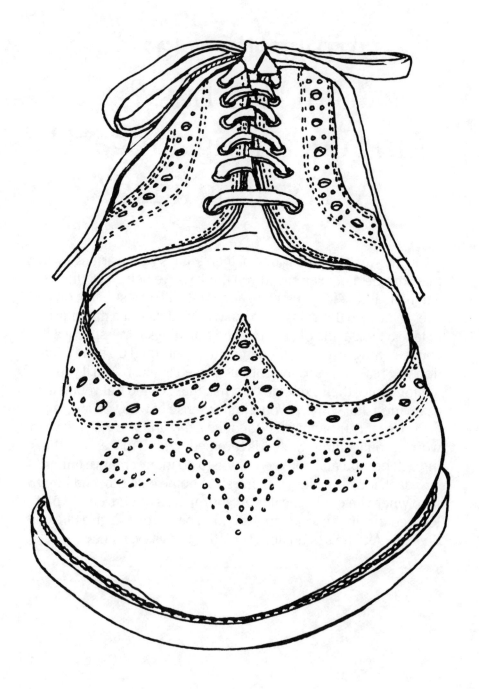

Final Thought

The only truly happy people are children and the creative minority.

—Jean Caldwell, Great-Grandmother

Throughout this book I've talked about the various roles of the creative process. One thing I haven't done, however, is address what the *product* of this process is. As a matter of fact, I've been somewhat vague about it. I've allowed you the reader to imagine whatever product you wish it to be whether it's the creation of a new company, a new recipe for chicken, a way to put on a more interesting meeting, or a new style of sculpture. Well, here I'll come clean with you. *The product of the creative process is you.*

Just as a rock in a stream is molded by the current that flows around it or a cliff-dwelling tree is shaped by freezing rain and thin air, we too are shaped by our environment: the language we speak, the economic system of which we're a part, the clothes we wear, the food we eat, the media that bombard us. All of these influence the way we think and who we are.

But unlike stream-smooth rocks or Alpine trees, we are free to choose some of the processes in which we immerse ourselves. If you choose to be involved in projects that stretch you creatively, that force you to explore, manipulate, evaluate, and act in challenging ways, then ultimately you will be the beneficiary. And that's the biggest kick of all.

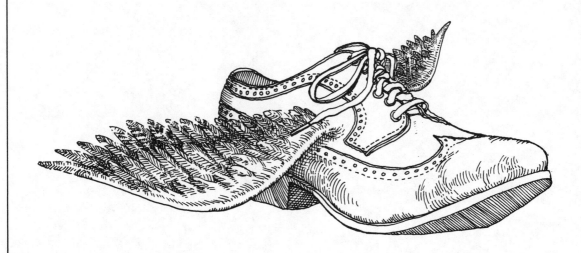

Back Matter

Notes

p. 6: One of the first to recognize this end-reversal phenomenon was Bill Gove.

p. 29: Answers to bionics exercise. 1-C, 2-H, 3-G, 4-I, 5-A, 6-B, 7-D, 8-J, 9-F, 10-E.

p. 31: Alan Kay. Presentation by Alan Kay at "Innovation In Industry" conference on March 26, 1985. Sponsored by Creative Think.

p. 32: Steve Jobs. Presentation by Steve Jobs at "Innovation In Industry" conference on October 7, 1981. Sponsored by Creative Think.

p. 56: Abraham Lincoln. This was based on work done at Bell Laboratories in the early 1970's to determine the least amount of information necessary for pattern recognition.

p. 57: National Library Week. Larry Dobrow, *When Advertising Tried Harder. The Sixties: The Golden Age of American Advertising.* New York: Friendly Press, 1984.

p. 68: "Switch horses."

p. 69: Carl Djerassi. Presentation by Dr. Djerassi at "Innovation In Industry" conference on November 2, 1982. Sponsored by Creative Think.

p. 75: A fun book on visual thinking is: Robert Sommer, *The Mind's Eye: Imagery in Everyday Life.* New York: Dell, 1978.

p. 82: Creativity test with comedy. James H. Austin, *Chase, Chase, & Creativity.* New York: Columbia University Press, 1978.

p. 84: Landscaping the paths. Christopher Williams, *Origins of Form.* New York: Architectural Book Publishing Company, 1981.

p. 96: Robert Gelber and timing. From John Dvorak's "Inside Track" column in *InfoWorld,* December 28, 1984.

p. 98: Sander Parallelogram. Peter Farb, *Humankind.* Boston: Houghton Mifflin, 1978.

p. 102: American Soldiers and Englishwomen. Paul Watzlawick, *How Real is Real? Confusion, Disinformation, Communication.* New York: Random House, 1976.

p. 131: Answers to positioning line exercise: 1-D, 2-F, 3-H, 4-G, 5-B, 6-A, 7-C, 8-E.

Index Of Proper Names

About The Author

Roger von Oech is the founder and president of Creative Think, a Menlo Park, California based company specializing in stimulating innovation and creativity in business. Creative Think provides consulting services, seminars, publications and conferences.

Prior to starting Creative Think in 1976, Roger was employed by IBM in the areas of data base and data communications. In addition, he has worked for Remington Rand in the Netherlands.

He is a Phi Beta Kappa graduate of Ohio State University, and earned his doctorate from Stanford University in a self-conceived program in the "History of Ideas."

He is married to Wendy (who also works for Creative Think) and they have two children, Athena and Alexander.

I hope you enjoyed this book. If you have any thoughts or comments or creative experiences you'd like to share, I would be delighted to hear from you. Address all correspondence to:

Creative Think
Box 7354
Menlo Park, California
94026